A Vilner, a Partisan
Repairing the Rent, Healing the Wounds
A Father Talks to His Son

Published in the United States by
Beckham Publications Group, Inc.
P.O. Box 4066, Silver Spring, MD 20914

ISBN: 978-0-9816505-7-9
0-9816505-7-0

10987654321

A Vilner, a Partisan
Repairing the Rent, Healing the Wounds
A Father Talks to His Son

Hirschka Varshavtchik's story
written by his son, Sidd Raichel

THE Beckham
PUBLICATIONS GROUP, INC.
PO BOX 4066, SILVER SPRING, MD 20914

Contents

Thank-yous abound:

To my father for opening his vault of memories.

To my mother for telling us, "You've talked for hours. *Ganuck* already," only to join in the shared memory, adding her perspective.

To my wife for reading and rereading the text, asking questions, piecing together strands of stories.

To my children for supporting me as I went off to that world for hours on end, days on end.

To my brothers for their encouragement and assistance throughout the process.

To Janice for transcribing the audio tapes as she learned to grapple with an East European accent.

To Mindle for transcribing the second interview.

To Ken for the artwork that graces this book's cover.

Dedicated to those who have survived—please tell your stories—and those who listen to and honor those reminiscences.

In Memory of those who did not—Boruch Eliahu and Sonya Varshavtchik, Lolkah Varshavtchik, Goldie Varshavtchik, Zalman and Sarah Raichel— each grandfather, each grandmother, each father, each mother, each uncle, each aunt, each brother, each sister—each and everyone with an untold story to tell

Prologue

I never knew my grandfathers:
not my mother's father, not my father's father.
I never knew my grandmothers:
not my mother's mother, not my father's mother.
Like most of my aunts and uncles,
like most of my cousins,
like most of my parents' childhood friends,
they were all killed
—killed during the unfathomable horrors of the Holocaust
—killed because. . .
because they were Jewish.

By the time I was born, in 1955, my parents had already settled into the fabric of America and were on their way to making a better life for themselves. I grew up knowing very little of their prior lives, their prior trials, and their prior world — which was first dismantled, then dismembered, and finally destroyed. Only in the decade before, they had been fighting for their own survival.

In a dark, dark cellar, locked in a small wooden chest, hidden in the most remote corner of my parents' minds, they had laid to an uneasy rest their life before America. I grew up with precious few stories of my parents or our extended family. My two older brothers, Barry and Sol, and I somehow knew we were to ask very little. My parents volunteered even less.

So, when the dreams came, when the ghosts came, I didn't have the words to frame the images swirling about me, calling out to me, sometimes even brushing up against my face—for those words had always remained unspoken. That small wooden chest, locked in that dark, dark cellar, could not withstand the press of memory, yearning to be free. So I witnessed the burning of villages. I saw the ovens of death blazing in all their wretched evil. I saw the long marches in the dead of winter. But I had no words with which to speak, to ask, to beg for understanding.

The first dream was of my maternal grandfather. I see his hands in recurring dreams to this day, but only his hands: manicured, gentle, yet strong. Zalman Raichel was a sculptor and a painter. He was an accomplished artist, commissioned to sculpt pieces for an international exposition in Argentina, in 1926. My mother was only two years old at the time, but she still remembers how her father loved Argentina. He actually suggested the family move there, but that would have taken them too far from the rest of their family. I often feel his presence. To honor him, I have taken Raichel as my pen name.

There have been other childhood dreams as well. I see myself hiding by stone stairs leading up to cobblestone streets from a basement apartment. I cringe as I hear the pounding of black boots marching across the cobblestones. I bolt, a frightened child, running blindly, not remembering the way, reaching a dead end, a barbed wire fence, caught by those shiny black boots; taken, beaten, tortured, not wanting to tell, not knowing if I had told, not knowing if my secrets remained hidden, not knowing even as I was killed. More of my dreams, many more, have been of this nature.

Walking around the house in the more rational light of day, the specters still hovered — restless, wanting. I saw them, but didn't have any words to set them free. I couldn't ask my parents because the images that haunted me were from a buried, wordless world.

And the holidays, whether somber as Yom Kippur, the Day of Atonement, my father standing to say the Mourner's Kaddish for so many, or as delightful as Chanukkah lighting up winter's darkest nights—each and every holiday was muddied by unspoken shadows. I remember being in our relatives Edie and Jack's house. My brothers and I played dreidel with Edie and Jack's three sons, Larry, Alan and Benjamin. Everyone was laughing enjoying the game, and, though I played too, I was caught in shadows, caught in the undercurrent of unspoken memories. Even the light and warmth of the Chanukkah menorah was dimmed, tainted by that unexpressed world in which I lived.

I grew up confused, surrounded by unuttered family memories I couldn't comprehend. I was all alone in this dark, dark place, where even language itself had failed me. Bits of family stories—true or not, it did not matter—came in hushed breaths. My brother told me once that we got our name Reischer because our father killed a German soldier and took his identity papers. I clutched to each new phrase as a precious piece of the puzzle to answer the questions: 'Where did I come from?' and 'Who am I?'

In the late 1960s, there were whispers of contact with Grisha, my mother's brother. He had been "liberated" by the Russians long ago, in that time of the lost world. Only he was found now, still living in Russia, and we could write. My parents were careful about what to say in each letter knowing that mail could be opened and censored.

I grew up quiet, a loner, with no real friends. My parents were worried about me. I graduated from high school in January 1971, just before I turned sixteen. So, before starting college the next fall, my parents sent me to Israel, to visit Uncle Yechial, my father's younger brother. They hoped the change of scene would ease my troubled silence.

As much as my parents kept their personal horrors locked in that wooden chest, Yechial talked. His chest of memories was laid wide open. My uncle spoke continuously of the life before, of the world lost, of the Holocaust he had survived. He brought me to Yad Vashem, Israel's Memorial to the six million Jews who had been killed. With only simple words—I knew precious little Hebrew, and had but an elementary understanding of Yiddish, while he spoke very little English—we walked from room to room and took in the stark images of the Holocaust. In front of a black stone floor map of Europe depicting where and how many Jewish people were murdered, understated but unmistakably clear, he pointed out to me where my grandparents had died, where Lolkah, my uncle, had died, where relatives whose names I had never been told had all lost their lives.

I cried for these people. I cried for my uncle who seemed so at ease with the burden of knowing. I cried for my parents and for my brothers. And I cried for myself, tears poured from eyes like twin rivers in flood. I knew that what I was being told, what I was coming to understand, no one…no one, regardless of circumstance, should ever have to endure. Yechial had given me many harsh pieces to the story of the lost world from which I had come. The images were all a jumble, but at least now for the first time, I was allowed, encouraged, even forced to view this world openly and put words to the terrors revealed.

My father and mother attended Holocaust survivors' reunions, both in New York City and in Israel. At one such gathering in Israel during the early 1980s, several of the speakers told those present to go home and tell their stories to their children. Menachem Begin, Israel's Prime Minister, spoke of the need to tell. One speaker, Abba Kovner, was one of my father's commanding officers. Because it was Abba Kovner, because it was his partisan commander, my father spoke to me when he came home.

My father told me one story. It was about the time my mother was paralyzed and almost lost her life. Afterward, he had nightmares for the next month. He apologized to me, saying he could tell me no more.

It was a few months later when he told me another story, a story about Yechial. A few months later, another story—on each occasion his nightmares returned, and after a time, receded again. Each story added pieces to the puzzle of my family's history. I was, for the first time, being given the words by which the images that had haunted me could be named, could be framed, could be contained.

Now, many years later, I asked my father to tell me his story, not just a "bissile" here a "bissile" there, but the whole story. And he said he would.

My father walked into the cellar of his memories and pulled out that chest. He thrust it open wide and reached in with both hands to give me those horrible, horrible treasures. To have lived it once was horrific beyond any words we can use to attempt an understanding. To be willing to share those buried memories takes great bravery. Once I heard his story I knew why he had been silent for so long.

Chapter 1: Early Memories

Zits mian kinnd, Sit my child. I will tell you my story. I was born on the sixth of June, 1922, in Vilna, which at that time was part of Poland. Vilna was a beautiful city. The Vileika flowed north through the center of the city, a stream in a valley, that joined the winding Vilia River. Vilna was surrounded on three sides by hills. The countryside was magnificent in every season.

Here is a map of Vilna, spelled Wilno. Kiena, which was the location of a summer home and a place relatives lived, is located to east by southeast of Vilna. The same Vileika River which runs through Vilna winds around to run through Kiena as well.

The Jewish quarter of the city was crowded; the narrow cobblestone streets were bustling with business. The Jewish quarter was in the center of the city. People spoke mainly Yiddish. There were quite a few outdoor markets, mostly farmers who came to the city to sell their crops. Also they sold eggs, milk, sour cream; all the dairy products. Farmers used to come from at least thirty kilometers away.

Vilna was both a very rich and a very poor city. The feeling was a richness of life, of a close caring community. But it was hard to make a living. My father worked hard and made a good living, but there was not enough work for all the Jewish families.

There were some industries in Vilna. The center of the fur industry in Poland was in Vilna. There was a radio factory called Elektrit. Most of the people were workers, shoe makers, tailors, cabinet makers, hard-working people.

You could feel when it was a holiday. All the stores were closed. People were dressed in fine clothes and went to the synagogue. All around you the city was filled with excitement. We were forty percent Jewish in Vilna. Most of the people were Orthodox Jews. Most of the people were religious. You had a Jewish life in Vilna.

At night the city was quiet. I remember there were electric street lights. On the streets were very few trees, but we had many large parks. Off the trees used to fall *kashstaanish,* chestnuts. In the winter they were sold hot on a plate. We used to go ice skating in the park called Bernadean's Garden. There were many chestnut trees there. We never went skiing though. Anything dangerous, my parents wouldn't let us do.

My mother, Sarah, Sonya they called her at home, was always beautiful, always dressed clean; just a pleasure to look at her. She used to go twice a week to the beauty parlor, for Shabbos and on Wednesday. Most of the time when we came home from school mommy would be wearing a white gown. She would be working behind the counter at the bakery downstairs. At home mommy would wear dresses. She wore long earrings and a wide necklace. She always wore rings as well. Mommy enjoyed dressing up.

My mother was dedicated to her children and my father's business. She wouldn't touch a bite before the kids were fed. She wouldn't buy for herself anything unless her kids had first. When there was a wedding and it came to cook the fish she was the head cook and the head waiter. I remember we used to go for *Pesach,* Passover, especially, to buy material for shirts and suits. First she got material for Lolkah, my older brother, then for Yechial, the youngest. Yeah, I was the third one when it came to clothes. Yechial was raised at home like a girl. My mother really wanted a girl. Yechial had long hair. He wore a very long coat. Everyone called him the *gallach,* the priest.

My father used to go for a haircut and a shave on Friday to the barber, up the hill. And one Friday, I remember it like today: Yechial was nine or maybe ten years old. My father took Yechial with him and the barber gave Yechial a man's haircut. After this he said, "You go home. I'll come a little later."

My mother was in the bakery behind the counter and Yechial walked in. We heard a bump, my mother fainted.

My father, Boruch Eliahu, lost both of his parents at an early age. When his father, Hirsh-Zvi, was on his deathbed in 1916, Boruch sat by his side. Hirsch-Zvi said to him, "Get off my bed. The *Malach Hamavet,* the Angel of Death, is coming in. He won't come until you leave."

Boruch said to his father, "Tell the *Malach Hamavet* that I had a dream. He should look on the other side of the page. It says you should have another day to live." Hirsch-Zvi told the Malach Hamavet to *"Drey ibber the zajtl."* Turn over the page. And he did live one more day.

My father was devoted to his mother, Rachel. After Hirsch-Zvi passed away Rachel became ill. My father would not marry until his mother passed away. Boruch also took care of all of his sisters. He was the only son. He didn't want a wife in the house to care for as well. Before passing away in 1918, his mother told him, "I'll always be with you."

My father was little on the heavy side, okay, maybe a lot on the heavy side. He was a very friendly man. He didn't wear a beard, but was not clean shaven. He used an electric razor. My father worked twelve to fourteen hours a day at the family bakery. The bakery was a corner store, at 41 Zavalna Street. He would wear a suit to work. He would oversee the workings of the bakery. We had about sixteen tables for people to sit and drink. This part of the business was like a coffee shop. It was a very hard business. My father used to get up, I think, at four o'clock in the morning, and closed the store around ten o'clock at night.

There were ten or more people working in the bakery: cake masters, a baker who made Kaiser rolls, and another baker just for bagels. I wasn't allowed in the back where the baking happened. My father had a counter built with a big opening to the back. We could see everything that was going on in the shop. We had a place to sit and watch and talk through this cutout, like a window.

We had four stores though all the baking was done at the main bakery on Zavalna Street. We had one store just across the street from the railroad station, a very good location. Here, my mother's younger sister, Edith, worked. Then we had another one, right across the street from the *halla,* the outdoor farmer's market. The fourth shop was in a Polish neighborhood. There we sold less bread, but more cake. We had Christian customers as well as Jewish customers.

Every Passover, the bakery was koshered. All the *chumitz,* the not kosher for Passover foods, were cleaned out of the bakery. Then different cakes and cookies were baked for Passover. *Matzah,* unleavened bread, was made in a separate place, a *matzah padraat,* a place to bake matzah.

The week before Passover, you had to walk on the ceiling at home. The floors were painted and polished. Everything was scrubbed, cleaned down to the tiniest crumb. That was how my mother got ready for Passover.

To celebrate Purim, like every holiday, we went to synagogue. Every time Hamin's name was mentioned the kids would shoot him with toy guns. For us at home and in the bakery, we used to prepare *humintoshin,* a three cornered cookie. For every holiday we had special foods. For Hanukkah we used to make *griebenesse,* the skin of a goose cooked with onions. We sold it in the store as well, and it was delicious.

Across the street from us was the Evangelist Church. Whenever there was a special service at the church my father sent over cakes and breads. He gave donations to the church. The priest was always kind to us. He would come and buy from the store, and stay and talk. His name was Ksiadz Jankowski. He was a good man. At that time he was in his sixties. He always wore the black gown. He wore a priest's hat to cover his gray-black hair.

My older brother, Lolkah, worked in the bakery. He started when he was fifteen years old. He didn't want to go to school so my father put him to work, and this is where he developed his muscles. Lolkah made dough from one hundred kilo sacks of flour. He had to mix it by hand. They had machines for mixing dough, but bread dough was mixed by hand.

Our apartment was right above the bakery. In the house, on every door frame, was a *mezuzah*, a small case holding the Shema, the central prayer of the Jewish religion. The mezuzah on the door to the outside was larger than the rest and made of copper. My parents had a bedroom; my aunt had a bedroom; Vera, our housekeeper had a room; Lolkah had a bedroom for himself; and Yechial and I slept in the living room on a foldout couch. We had a very large living room with a lot of plants at the end of the living room by the windows. I would say maybe sixty plants. And my mother used to take care of them, wash and clean and water them, and watch them for every leaf, the plant should be healthy.

The dining room table was as big as a Ping-Pong table, and we used to play Ping-Pong on this table. The table had, if I'm not mistaken, twelve or fourteen chairs. Above the table was a big chandelier; a lot of crystal. There was a sideboard as you came into the room. On the right side was a china cupboard, just for silver. We even had silver plates. On the left side was a sideboard that was strictly for Pesach, for Passover. Dishes, Rosenthal dishes, and pots were stored in this buffet.

Vera was our housekeeper ever since I could remember. My father found her as a young girl in White Russia on the road and took her in after his parents had both passed away. Vera was like one of the family. She was raised in our house, then became a maid. When she married, her wedding was in our house. When she had a son the three of them all lived in our house.

Not everybody in Vilna had hot water, but we did. The hot water boiler that we heated with wood stood by the bathtub. Later my parents remodeled the house to have the heating done by coal, but the bathtub boiler was still heated by wood.

The apartment faced out into a courtyard. There were steps by the back of the bakery to go out. We lived to the right. Tefka and Yechial Sheers and their parents, a family of nine in all, lived to the left. Their apartment was just above our bakery ovens. They never had to heat the house, but in the summer, it was a torture.

Our house, our apartment, we had to heat and that's why it was remodeled. An oven was put in the wall in such a way that four rooms could each be heated up at the same time. At the end of our apartment there was a big, big pantry to hold food; canned stuff, glass jars, barrels, just a pantry, but it was tremendous.

And this was what we kept in the winter. Kraut. In the summer we kept the pickles. We put away the apples for the winter. I remember they used to pack the apples in newspaper and store them in crates.

When I was nine, maybe ten, about five of us came to my house. Alex Kremer and Michoyale Kovner were two of the boys. We closed the door in the apartment, and we lit up cigarettes. We sat in the living room with all the doors closed. Certainly when five people smoke, it got kind of thick, you know. Somebody came to the bakery and hollered to my father that he saw smoke in the house. My father ran up the stairs and caught us smoking.

So first of all, he said that we were doing it wrong. He took us outside on the balcony. He said, "You can't smoke in the house. You have to smoke here; otherwise you can start a fire." He went down to the store and bought five cigars. He made us all smoke the cigars—and we all got so sick.

Summers were spent in the country, in a town called Kiena, about twenty kilometers from Vilna. I had two aunts there, Brina and Rejzele. The older one was Brina. She had no children and she had a sick husband. He died of cancer. I remember when the doctor came and said he couldn't do anything for him. He explained to my father that the surgeon had opened Brina's husband up like opening a vest, but the cancer had spread everywhere, and there was nothing the surgeon could do. I was about ten years old at the time. We couldn't go the cemetery for the funeral. If you had living parents you weren't allowed to go the cemetery. Whenever we used to go to visit Brina, she was in seventh heaven every time we came into her house.

In the country, in Kiena, we went swimming every day in the Vilia River, the same river that flowed by Vilna. We went camping at least twice a week, three times a week. My father used to come on Friday, stay Saturday, and leave either late Saturday, or on Sunday morning back to Vilna by train from Kiena.

If my father couldn't come he sent word to us. I don't remember how, but he used to let us know if he was sending food: bakery goods, cakes, from Vilna, from the bakery, to the country. I really don't remember how he contacted us, by telephone, by word of mouth, somehow.

We did have a telephone in Vilna. Not all the houses had telephones but we did. I remember making my first call. I was ten years old. I called a girl.

When she picked up the phone and said hello, I felt a lump in my throat. I waited, and then, finally hung up. I remember it like today.

We also used to come and stay with my aunts in Kiena in the winter. This is when Yechial fell into a barrel of sauerkraut. He was reaching in for some kraut, reaching further and further until, in he went. He was maybe six, maybe five. Yechial was born in '25, so this must have been 1930.

In Vilna there were public schools and Hebrew schools, which were private schools. We went to a Hebrew school for our education. One school was called *Tarbut* located on Zavanya Street number 2. Another school was *Tushio*, which was much closer to the house. I went to Tushio until the fourth grade. Then I went to Tarbut until seventh grade. Tarbut was a big school, a three story building with a lot of children. There, besides learning Polish and all the subjects, we also learned Hebrew. I dreamt of being an engineer at that time, but the war broke out and that was the end of the schooling.

The principals of both schools were brothers, Gerebitch was their last name. Wherever you walked in school you saw signs *Dabeir Evrit, Dabeir Evrit,* Speak Hebrew, Speak Hebrew. Classes were taught in Polish and Hebrew, not Yiddish. In the house my parents spoke only Yiddish.

For school I used to wear a neat shirt and shorts with long stockings, just below the knee. In the winter I wore longer pants that went just below the knee. I would tie them with a string. I wore short socks and the lower part of my legs were uncovered.

Every Friday night and Saturday, and every holiday, we attended synagogue with my father: every Shabbos, men on one side, women on the other. It was the synagogue of the bakers, located on German Street, just a block away from the main synagogue in Vilna. The synagogue was in an apartment building nearby. The synagogue was one big square room with seats. In front of the seats was a place where you could put your *siddur,* prayer book; the same as all over Europe.

The *Bima,* where the rabbi stood, was very holy and *Oren,* the arc that held the Torah, was the holiest. When a new torah was written, it was like a wedding, with dances, music, and fiddlers. My father was a *gabbi,* a torah reader, and a member of the board of directors. He sat facing everyone, on the bima by the *mitzrock* wall, the wall facing Jerusalem. There were two long benches with cushions on the bima. There were wooden stands for you to place the prayer book on. There were forty or so members of the synagogue. Mostly just the men came to the Shabbos service. It was on the High Holidays that both the men and the women came.

My father was a very religious man. As well as being a gabbi, he used to attend Yeshivahs and study with scholars. He used to help poor scholars be able to sit and learn. When poor scholars found a girl and couldn't afford a wedding, we used to have weddings in our home. My father donated all the food for the wedding. When he was in concentration camp, during Passover he and the rabbi collected a little bit flour and baked matzoh at night. I learned this after the war.

Vilna was known as the Jerusalem of Lithuania. There were over one hundred thirty synagogues in the city. The large city synagogues were amazing sights, tall ceilings held by wide stone pillars, services for hundreds and hundreds of people. The main synagogue, the Vilna City Synagogue, was magnificent. It was called simply the Great Synagogue. The ceiling was domed, with balconies in the rear. The men sat downstairs and women sat in the balcony. Hugh pillars held up the roof. The world's greatest cantors would come to this synagogue. It was a great honor for a cantor. The tzefilin was used by men in prayer and worship. The cover of the tzefilin was made out of silver. The *tzefilin* was worn on the forehead and around the hand. My father had my tzefilin waiting for me to use for years. Until the *Bar Mitzvah,* when you were acknowledged as an adult at the age of thirteen in the Jewish community, you practiced how to put on tzefilin, how to make the *shadiah* on your finger. After your Bar Mitzvah, you prayed with tzefilin every morning before you went to school. My Bar Mitzvah was in the summer. I remember getting a lot of presents, books and fountain pens.

Around the age of twelve, before my Bar Mitzvah, I joined Bet Trumpledor, called Beitar, a political party. There were different political organizations in Vilna. Beitar believed that military force should be used to create a Jewish homeland in the Middle East. I joined because I believe we had to fight for a homeland and because I had friends in Beitar. Yechial had more friends from Shomer Ha'tzair. They believed in buying land from the Arabs to create a Jewish State. Abba Kovner was in this political group. They believed in negotiating with the Arabs. Lolkah was too busy with girls to join a political group.

I knew your mother from this time. First of all, I knew Fanya's brother Grisha, and then, for a few years, from 1934 to 1936, we went on dates. Three boys and three girls, always in groups, and somehow, Fanya was the youngest and would always be there. We would go to dances, and they always ended up in fights between the Beitar group and the Shomer Ha'tzair group. But it was good natured arguments. We were all classmates. It was a good life.

Chapter 2: Rising Anti-Semitism

By 1938 anti-Semitism was very high. There were demonstrations, people carrying signs saying *Swooy do Sweg,* "Buy by Your Own," meaning don't buy from the Jews. One student stood in front of the bakery with such a sign. When the priest, Ksiadz Jankowski, saw this, he came out of the church and called to the people in the street not to listen, to come into the bakery and buy there.

This happened many times. It was mostly Polish students who would stand in front of the store telling gentiles not to buy from Jews. The priest, whenever he saw this, came out to chase them away. He would be the first one to come into the store.

Even before 1938 we faced anti-Semitism. When I was eleven or twelve, we were in the country. Vera and her son came with us. They were sitting on the porch and he was refusing to eat. I overheard Vera saying in Polish, "If you don't eat, a Jew with a long beard will come and cut your throat to use your blood for matzah." This was Vera, raised in our house. She spoke Yiddish better than me. She was with my family since before we children were born. I thought this was some kind of joke so I told the story in school. My teacher told me, "Forget it, and never repeat it!" I was too young to understand what it all meant.

In Vilna there were colleges and universities. There were Jewish schools and public schools. Katanah-berezah was a public university. There came out a law that Jewish students had to sit on the left side of the classroom. Then a law was passed stating that ninety percent of the students had to be Polish before Jewish students could be let in. There were more and more restrictions.

When a Jewish student was supposed to go to the army he was to join as an officer. But then the Polish didn't want too many Jewish officers so Jews were rejected from the army. It was called "*naglitch-bov-ay,* too many by the numbers."

We had an uncle in Warsaw, Uncle Lable, and an uncle in Africa, Uncle Mottle. Both of them were my mother's brothers. We called Uncle Lable, Eelick the Dark. He had two children. Anytime Uncle Lable was in trouble, he wrote either to my mother, or to her sisters Itke or Rikle. And Itke or Rikle ran to our house and showed mommy the letter. Then they whispered that nobody should hear what kind of problems Uncle Lable had. This happened after Poland was divided between Germany and Russia.

So mommy and my aunts used to send packages, thin wooden boxes that they would cover with linen. But the packages that were allowed could only weigh two kilograms. What could you put in a two kilogram package, a jar of honey? Raisins, I remember them packing up, some dried vegetables, to send. These packages were sent to the children in the Warsaw ghetto.

Once came a letter and I overheard my mommy speaking. I thought she said Uncle Lable went to work in the chemical plant and they might not see him anymore. The mother, Lable's wife, was taken to another chemical plant, and my mother and aunts didn't think they would see either of them anymore. So the only ones who were left in the house were the little boy with his sister.

At the time we children didn't know what it was all about. They didn't print in the newspapers, about killing in concentration camps. We didn't know anything about it. These letters came at the end of 1938.

Then came a letter that the children wrote saying they hadn't seen their parents for a long time. They hadn't seen, for a month already, the butcher. And it had been two weeks since anyone had seen the baker. The letters made no sense to us kids when we overheard bits and pieces of the hushed conversations.

As my mommy and my aunts read the letter, and we children eavesdropped, we thought this was some kind of a joke; what, had Eelick changed jobs? But what the aunts meant in their quiet talking was, the family has no meat, they have no fish, they have no bread. Our parents understood this better than us, but they didn't tell us what's going on. Life was so bad there and the children were suffering. We heard that our Eelick the Dark had been taken to a gas factory. We didn't know what a gas factory was. We didn't understand that he had been killed.

Then later, when the Germans came to us, to Vilna, we lost contact and we didn't know what happened to the kids. If they survived…we never heard from them anymore.

Approximately a month before the war started in Vilna, during June of 1939, the Polish police arrested my father as a German spy because it was on record that in 1914, he had two million German marks in his house. He had been arrested as a spy back in 1914, but was later found to be innocent of any crime. In 1939, I don't know how, the Polish authorities dug up those papers. So the police came to the house and arrested my father as a German spy. They sent him to Katuz-Bereza, a prison. He was there for seven weeks. It was mostly for political prisoners. This prison was part prison, part concentration camp. The walls were very high. The gates were made of steel as were the cells. There were police everywhere and police dogs too. The guards were brutal. The worst prison to escape from was Katuz-Bereza.

My father saw his mother in a lot of dreams, in life-saving dreams. After he escaped from prison, he told us this story. He said, "It was in the middle of the night. My mother came to me in a dream and she said, 'Why are you laying here? Get up and get out.' I woke up, I looked around, it was very quiet in the prison, and I went to lie down and go back to sleep. I was thinking what does this mean? My mother tells me to get up and get out. How can I get up and get out?

"So I got up and looked around. Sure enough, the prison guards were gone. There were none to be seen anywhere in the prison. The cells were unlocked. We were fifty in the cell. We opened the door and walked out. All the prisoners escaped the cell."

The cells of the prisons were unlocked, but the main gate was still locked. No one could leave the grounds until the Russians came. When the Germans invaded Poland from the west the Russians came into Poland from the east, and Vilna became a part of Russia. The Russians came to the prison and set up, right away, a committee to oversee the prison. Before my father walked out of Katuz-Bereza, he tried to get the things that were taken away from him when he came into prison; his wedding band, his watch, and other possessions. All these things were returned to him. The committee also gave him a document stating that he was released from prison. With this document, he returned to Vilna.

The Russians and the Polish, at least in this area, hated each other. So when the Russians settled in Vilna, and here's an ex-prisoner from Katuz-Bereza, my father was like a hero. That's why we, as a family, had no problems with the Russians.

When the Russians came to liberate Vilna from Poland, they took away Elektrit, the radio factory. They picked up all the equipment on trucks, the whole factory. Any of the workers who worked in the factory went to Russia. The same thing with the students of the music school in Vilna; that's how they took your uncle, Fanya's brother, Grisha. I don't know if Fanya's parents knew, or if they gave their okay. Or if, without their okay, the Russians took him. They took the artists, the engineers, and the musicians. The Russians "liberated" them. The wealthiest people were also taken away to Russia. On the one hand, all these people were taken away, but on the other hand all of them survived the war.

When the Russians came in they had pockets full with rubles, Russian currency. They bought everything and anything you could imagine. Show them a book of matches, they bought it. Show them an English cigarette, they bought it.

Whatever you showed them, oh…they needed, they needed. Shoes, they needed. Boots, they needed. Leather; there wasn't a thing that they didn't need. Let's say it was worth twenty rubles, ask them for one hundred rubles; no problem, they gave you, right away, the money.

Before the war, we didn't know much about Russia because it was a closed frontier. Nobody could go to Russia and come back. When the Russians came in with so many rubles, so much money, you felt like all of Vilna became rich. You could go out and buy because you had so much money. You could buy things.

When we met up with the soldiers in the street, we asked, "What do you have in Russia?" They said they have everything, everything, they have in Russia!

So one of us asked, "Do you have bananas in Russia?"

"Oh, do we have bananas! We have a factory near Moscow that works 24 hours a day that manufactures bananas."

They didn't even know what a banana was. And one friend said, "Do you have *dales* in Russia?"

"We have so much *dales* in Russia. It's everywhere, and if you go to Russia you will get it too!" a soldier said.

And we laughed and laughed. *Dales* means poverty in Hebrew. My friend said, "He's finally telling the truth!"

In the spring of 1940, I met *Tavarish Natchalnik*, his title means Comrade

Captain. His name was Piekarnia Voyentorga. He was a captain in the Supply Division of the Russian army. He was in charge of procuring supplies. My father signed a contract with him. The store was now owned by the Russian army. A wooden sign was put up saying, "The bakery from Tavarish Natchalnik Piekarnia Voyentorga, the Russian army."

Tavarish Natchalnik Piekarnia Voyentorga was in Vilna for three months. I called him Tavarish Natchalnik, Comrade Captain.

Tavarish Natchalnik was in charge of the soldiers' supermarket. He was about my size; he was blond and older than me. He must be, then he was thirty-five, maybe. He bought for the army, and also he bought and sold on his own; cigarettes, rolls, cookies, cake. But sometimes he had nice things like clothes, shoes, or boots.

Tavarish Natchalnik came to our bakery at least twice a day. My father baked for the Russian army. Tavarish Natchalnik would come in for breads, rolls and some Danish. We loaded the baked goods on a piece of canvas on the truck and he covered it up. Then he drove the goods to Russian restaurants. His truck was like a little department store on wheels.

Tavarish Natchalnik taught me how to drive his little truck, how to steer, how to shift gears. He would come into the store and give me the keys. He taught me in the backyard of the bakery. I drove forward and backward. Once I almost broke his truck. I backed up into a ditch. We called a lot of guys to lift the back end out of the ditch. Afterwards, whenever he came to the bakery, he teased me about driving.

Soon after the Russians came into Vilna, they gave it away to Lithuania. Even after this happened the Russian soldiers stayed. The day before the Lithuanians came into the city, it was during November, there was a shortage of food and fuel. I remember in the bakery, it just happened that we had no flour, and we had no wood to heat the ovens. We couldn't bake. We had nothing to bake. It wasn't just us; the same thing was in different bakeries. So, certainly, there was a shortage in bread.

The Polish people started making a pogrom, a riot against us, against the Jews. There were maybe, let's say 2,000 people with hammers and shovels and whatever. And they came into the Jewish section of the city. Anything they saw, they broke. They broke the windows. They broke doors, they looted from stores.

The very next day, the Lithuanians came. I remember, across from our house was the police station. The Lithuanians took over the police station. The Lithuanian police were all at least six footers and they wore very tall hats with feathers on top. So they looked like seven footers. The Polish people were coming down the street; they turned right in front of our bakery. There was a policeman on one side of the street and a policeman on the other side of the street. When they heard the mob, the rest of the policemen came out from the precinct. The police stood with rifles on their shoulders. Otherwise, the crowd would have broken our windows. Everybody blamed the Jews for the shortages.

The second day of the Lithuanians being in charge of the city, they opened two warehouses: one for dairy and meat called Pinocentras, and one for groceries and goods called Latukes. Certainly, they brought food in from Kovna, Lithuania.

It wasn't an easy job for the Lithuanians because the Russians, when they came in, changed the railroad track. They used a wider railroad car than the rest of Europe so the Lithuanians had to transfer supplies from the narrow railroad car to the wider Russian car. So things, for example like salt, they had to shovel, because the salt was loose in the boxcar. They had to take it out from the narrow car and load it into the wider car—it was double the work. The same with flour, the same with cement, whatever was in bags. The same with the meat that came in coolers. The Lithuanians had to transfer it from the train cars riding the small track to the Russian train cars on the wider track.

My father was told to come to this warehouse—not to buy—to take. They didn't talk about money. "Come and get it. Just bake. Just do." The Lithuanians were helping the people of Vilna to have enough food. The Lithuanian government had the best politicians in the world. They sent in so much food, so much food that you can't imagine.

The next day, there was enough food; the very next day. The Lithuanians brought in wood. "Just take it. Just load it up, come with cars. Just take it." We went to Latukes with five wagons pulled by horses. We loaded up with flour; with everything we needed to bake. We loaded up wagons with salt, bags of salt. We had so much extra salt, we sold it in Russia fifty kilometers away, and seventy kilometers from Vilna to Bellarus.

The winter was very cold. The first police precinct was just across the street.

This was the largest precinct in Vilna. The police used to come into the bakery just to stay warm. So that's why we became very friendly with them. And they didn't take nothing for nothing. The police always paid for everything. If they were hungry they came to us to eat. We never charged them a nickel. We never charged them and they always paid. At night, they came to sit, to drink coffee or tea, to warm up. They were always welcome. This was how my father became friendly with the captain and the lieutenants.

The captain of Lithuanian police had exit visas that Jews who were fleeing from the west needed to cross the border into Russia. The documents would allow Jewish refugees to travel through Russia to Japan. Since the police knew my father they asked him to spread the word that exit visas were for sale. My father was the one who supplied the police with customers. There were no secrets. You didn't have to announce it to a newspaper.

I used to sit in the living room. Families came in and bought exit visas. The captain got paid for this, and I'm sure my father made a dollar on it. Most of the Jews who escaped from the west had plenty of money, but even if they didn't have, my father still gave the papers. That was how refugees tried to escape the war.

Our family discussed leaving Vilna. My father had family in America. My brothers and I wanted to go to Israel. I was a member of Beitar. Yechial was part of Shomer Ha'tzair. But business was so good that my parents didn't want to leave. My father had little interest in Zionism and he wasn't really interested in America either. He said, "I have America here right in Vilna."

As the capital of Lithuania, Vilna became a *ganayden*, a paradise. Anything in the world you could get in Lithuania. It was a change like overnight. People coming from the east didn't have where to eat. We were always busy, the profits were better than ever.

There were no restrictions on the Jewish people under Lithuanian control. We had freedom. There was no religious persecution.

We heard horror stories from those families coming from the west, but we just didn't believe those stories. It was too unbelievable to imagine.

We never thought, in our worst nightmares, we never thought such things could happen. With Russia watching over Lithuania, we felt safe from Germany. We never thought they would come into Vilna.

Chapter 3: The Germans Take Over Vilna

Approximately three weeks before Germany declared war on Russia, in June of 1941, my father was arrested by the Russians, because he gave flour to make *matzah*, the bread of affliction eaten during the Passover holiday. My father gave a one hundred kilo bag of flour to someone in the courtyard so that he could take it to a matzah *padraat*, a special baker, to make matzah. Since the bakery was now owned by the Russian government the flour was no longer my father's to give.

So, for the second time, my father was sent to prison. My mother went there and stood outside in the street every morning around eight o'clock. He rose to the window to see her and wave. One morning, he waved goodbye and shouted down to her that the Russians were emptying the prison. He would be taken to Russia. There were four floors in the prison. He was on the top floor. The Russians evacuated the prisoners from lower three floors, but the ones on the top floor they left behind. They didn't have enough train cars to take the last of the prisoners out to Russia.

But my mother didn't know this. So she left the house and she traveled by truck on the way to Russia. She thought she would meet him there some place; that she would somehow find him in Russia. How she thought she would do this, I have no idea.

Before we knew that my mother had left, my brother, Lolkah, and his fiancé, Jenke, and I were already at the railroad station, in the car on the train bound for Russia. We wanted to escape the Germans. The only way to escape them was to go east.

My aunt, who knew where we were, came to the station and told us that my father had come home, but my mother had not. She had gone to Russia.

So, Lolkah and Jenke remained on the train and I returned home to see my father. The train took them as far as Minsk, the capital of Belerusia, but the Germans had already reached Minsk first. The front was already maybe one hundred or two hundred kilometers further east. The Germans had already come this far into Russia. You couldn't go any further. And that's how Lolkah came into the Minsk *lager*, labor camp. He was arrested because he was a man. All the men were taken to the lager, Jews and non-Jews. Jenke they sent free; she managed to make her way back to Vilna.

Overnight, the Germans took over Vilna. The Russian army had retreated before the German onslaught. During the first two days of the German occupation my father ran his store just like normal. He made a lot of money because the German currency was worth more than the Lithuanian currency. When a German soldier came into the store he would wait on line just like anyone else, but he would pay in German marks. On the third day of the occupation, early in the morning it was, near the end of June, a German officer and a Lithuanian policeman came into the bakery and they said to my father, "Mr. Varshavtchik, we are arresting you."

"Why? What did I do?" my father asked.

"We want your business. We don't need you so you are under arrest." Just like this, no reason given, no reason needed. "We're taking over the store." And, "You're under arrest," they said to my father. "Not only are you under arrest, we are taking you with us, and we are sending you to Ponary where you will be shot."

So my father said to them, "Can I please go up and say goodbye to my children?"

My mother wasn't home. She was still looking for my father; she was traveling back from Russia. But upstairs, in the house, it was only Yechial and me. Lolkah was still in Minsk.

My father came out from the back door. Instead of going up the steps to the house, he went into the yard, to the street, and across into the church. He was hidden by Ksiadz Jankowski, the priest. For three hours my father hid in the rafters. Ksiadz Jankowski was questioned by the Germans. Even though the priest said my father wasn't there, they searched the church. After three hours my father escaped to Kiena, but Yechial and I knew nothing of this.

At 5:30 in the morning, we heard a knock on the door. It was opened and certainly we saw a German officer and a Lithuanian policeman standing with their guns. They told us to get dressed. Yechial and I quickly put on pants and shoes. The two of them took us to the police station across the street, and locked us in a cell. Yechial was only seventeen at the time. I was nineteen. We had no idea what was going on.

The Lithuanian policeman said to us, "Where is your father?"

I said, "I don't know, in the bakery."

"No he is not. He was there, but he is not anymore."

I said, "I'm sorry, I don't know. I have no idea."

They left us locked in the cell.

Another Lithuanian policeman came in. He looked at us and he said nothing. He just looked at us. We knew him and he knew us because the bakery was right across the street. He used to come in during the winter to warm up.

Ten minutes later, this policeman opened the cell and filled it up with maybe twenty Jews. This policeman, and another policeman whom we also knew, had brought them in off the street and into the cell. Five minutes later, those two policemen opened up the cell again, and chased us all out into the street. Yechial and me, too.

In the street, there was already a crowd of people lining up to turn in their radios. Everybody who had been in the cell had to take a radio or two from a pile depending on the size of the radio. It was a mountain with radios. We had to form a line, stay in line. We joined the crowd already in the street, lined up in four rows, and the police marched us to the city hall where we all turned in the radios, and then we could walk away, free.

But it shows you, this Lithuanian policeman who recognized us knew exactly what was going on and why we were in the cell. He filled it up with other people, and took us all out together to turn in radios so my brother and I could sneak out with the crowd and be free.

On the way back home, just by the corner of our house, two Lithuanians, we called them *Chapner Ketchers*, Jew Catchers, were standing. One called me over and he said to me, "Are you Jewish or Polish?"

I didn't want to leave Yechial by himself, so I said, "I'm Jewish."

The same thing the other guy asked Yechial. "Are you Jewish or Polish?"

And Yechial said, "I'm Jewish," because he didn't want to leave me alone. You know we should have planned for something like this, but we hadn't and didn't know what else to do.

So they sent us into the square to join a group. They were catching Jews on the street and putting them in columns. About one hundred people were there already. They took us to the railroad station. It was about three kilometers, a good three kilometers.

In Lithuania when Chapner Ketchers caught a Jew, either they took him to Ponary or to work. The Chapner Ketchers accumulated one hundred people, one hundred Jews at a time. We were caught for work.

There were railroad cars loaded with bags of cement. We had to take the bags off the car and carry them inside a warehouse. With the bags we made steps so we could pile it very high. We had to walk up the cement bag steps to unload.

The curfew was, I think, eight o'clock. We finished unloading our car by 7:30. They took our group, whoever had been there, like twelve or fourteen people from this railroad car, and said go home. When I came home it was maybe ten minutes after the curfew already. But my aunt, my mother's youngest sister, Itke, who lived in our house, was waiting for us inside the gate. She opened the door and let us in. We were covered in cement dust from head to foot. We had to bathe right away.

Itke had a little note from my father written with a pencil that said, "I'm well, I'm going to Kiena." That's it. He had given the note to the priest, Ksiadz Jankowski. The priest came and gave it to my aunt.

With the Germans in Vilna, I stayed in the house with Yechial and my Aunt Itke. We hid there. We didn't go out any more. We were not in hiding, but we didn't leave the apartment. We sat in the house. Whatever food we had was enough. We couldn't go out and buy anything. We ate only whatever we had prepared.

The German soldier and the Lithuanian policeman never came. They never came again. The bakery was opened and run by someone, not us. We didn't know what happened. After five days it was closed.

After a week, my mother came home. She had traveled to Gluboki. I think that was the name of the town on the border between Poland and Russia. She wasn't allowed into Russia. The Germans were already going further into Russia, so she had nowhere else to go. She had to come back. She was so happy and relieved to know that father was nearby in Kiena.

My mother decided to walk to Kiena to find my father. She reached there without any problems. My father wasn't in the house with his sister. He was five kilometers away. He was working on the *Torf*, on a dig. He dug in the swamps. The mud was squeezed through a machine and stacked into bricks, like a pyramid. The bricks were left to dry in the air.

He was in a *lager*, a labor camp. He lived in a big barracks. In the barracks were about two hundred people. There was only one guard, but the prisoners or laborers, whatever you call them, were responsible if somebody ran away. If somebody ran away the guard shot ten workers, so they themselves were watching that nobody should run away.

Our father said we should all come to Kiena. My mother returned to Vilna. She took all the jewelry and money we had. My mother secured it very well, wrapped it in cloth bags and stored it all in a leather pouch. Then she returned to Kiena and my parents buried the pouch in the ground near my aunt's house. My father was still afraid to come back to Vilna, so my mother thought she would come back to Vilna to take the children to Kiena.

My father was in a labor camp, but we could live in my aunt's house. We could be together, close to one another. That's the way the brain worked at that time, thinking what to do to survive. We weren't sure what we would do, but at least we would be close together. You couldn't make plans for the future. Maybe we would ask a gentile family to hide us. We didn't know. My mother and father were trying to keep the family together somehow.

The same day that my mother came back from Kiena, after planning to move the family, there was a proclamation. Tomorrow everybody had to go to ghetto. The Germans announced the city of Vilna was closed. So Mother didn't want to take the chance with the children to go to Kiena.

Also on this day, Lolkah came home. He had plenty of stories to tell. In Minsk, in the lager, labor camp, a Lithuanian delegation came to take out Lithuanian citizens who had been detained. Many Lithuanians stepped forward to be freed. So whoever was Lithuanian got "RELEASED FROM MINSK LABOR CAMP" stamped on his passport, and was sent home.

One Jewish boy, a Lithuanian, went also to the same commission. A Lithuanian official looked at his passport, saw "Zhvidas", took out a gun and shot him, right there on the spot, in front of everyone. "Zhvidas" meant Jew in Lithuanian.

After the commission left, there were six Vilna boys, all of them Jewish, that spoke to the German commander of the prison. They said they had just come from work, and they heard the Lithuanian commission had been here. They showed their passports and asked to be returned to Lithuania. The German commander could not read Lithuanian. He saw the Lithuanian emblem on the passports, "The Republic of Lithuania" so he knew the passports were legitimate. He didn't see the German "Jedus" stamped on the passport, only the Lithuanian "Zhvidas", so he stamped "Bafrayt als Lager Minsk", freed from the Lager Minsk, on their passports. Then he signed his name by the stamp to make it official, and that's how these six came home to Vilna. Lolkah was one of these six boys.

What he saw coming from Lager Minsk to Vilna opened everyone's eyes to what was going on. He saw the way they were shooting the people for nothing, for sneezing. All the stories we had refused to believe, we now wondered if they were true.

And that day we also found out that he was married. Jenke's parents had known, but this was when we found out.

Mother was with us for more than a day. She didn't go to father. We were busy taking out all the clothes, the furs, the dresses, and bringing them to two places. The biggest part of the clothing went to a very rich guy called Antonovitch. He had a very big liquor store about three blocks away from us. They were going back and forth with material, with dresses, with bundles of clothing. We hoped to get some of the clothes back to trade with farmers for food, but Antonovitch gave us nothing, not one crumb. Instead of holding the clothing for us, he traded them away for himself.

A smaller portion of the clothing we took to the church across the street. We trusted the priest very much. However, we also didn't get anything in return for the clothes we gave to the priest. But this we know for a fact, the Germans came into the church and took away whatever the priest had been given.

Later, at the end of 1941, Beyonka Yakabon, a friend of mine, who worked in the Gestapo headquarters, brought me a brown jacket of cloth and wool. It was my very own jacket from our house from before the war that we had left with the priest. So, we knew the Germans had taken it.

A month after the German takeover, we had to wear a white cloth with a yellow circle and the letter "J" to show that we were Jewish. If you were not wearing the "J" you could be shot. The "J" was worn on the chest, on the left side. Another one was worn on your back, also on the left side. The "J" had to be worn on the outside of whatever you wore. Every time a new SS officer was in charge, the symbol changed, which was quite often. Eventually we had to wear the yellow Star of David on our jacket.

We weren't allowed to walk on the sidewalk. We had to walk in the street. There were no newspapers, no radios. The only news was word of mouth and who knew what was rumor and what was true. The synagogues were closed.

When we came into the ghetto, the whole family had to live in one big room. It was an apartment of two or three rooms, I don't remember; maybe two rooms and a little kitchen. So our family took one room, and another family took the other room. There were all three sisters; Rickla, Itke and my mommy, plus Rickla's husband, Abrasha, and their son Eelick, Lolkah and his wife Jenke, and Yechial and me. Also Jenke's parents were there too, all in one room.

You could bring in only what you could carry on you. The rest of your possessions were left in the house. So many valuables left behind for anyone to take. In our courtyard were many Jewish families and only two gentile families. For the gentiles this was like a holiday.

In one way though it was easier in the ghetto. You could walk around without fear of being arrested or shot.

My mother wanted to see my father in Kiena. Abrasha worked in a German garage where they fixed trucks. He arranged with a German soldier that they would drive the truck to Kiena. Whether my mother decided to stay or to come back with my father, in either case Abrasha would return the truck. But, at the same time, Abrasha wanted to organize so that we should be able to get some food.

Where he worked and later, where my father worked too, was a unit that fixed trucks. The Germans had taken over the whole building. In the yard they fixed trucks, but they also removed all the people from the apartment building. So Abrasha with the German soldier went into the apartments and took out bundles of clothing. They put it on the truck.

Abrasha came to the ghetto with the truck. He took my mother and they drove to Kiena. The German soldier agreed because he wanted to go to the country and trade the clothing with the farmers for potatoes, eggs, cheese, a fresh vegetable, a tomato, a cucumber—whatever.

The night before my mother set out, my father had a dream. He said it was in the middle of the night. His mother came to him in dream again and said,

"*Vos ligstu do?* Why are you lying here? Get up and get out. Run away. Get up and get out!"

He told us he got up, walked outside, but it was very quiet. My father said, "There is something wrong. It cannot be." So he went back inside and went to sleep.

His mother came to him again, saying, "I told you, get up and get out. Get out from this lager!"

So my father got up. He put on a pair of pants and went outside. He went behind a pyramid of clay bricks. In about five minutes the barracks were surrounded by Lithuanian and German soldiers as well as the gentiles of the town. They gathered up all the Jewish workers, as my father slipped away. While he was walking he heard a little boy crying. The boy had been separated from his parents. My father came to the boy. Later, we found out it was Solkah Defishikah's son. So he grabbed this little boy and said, "Come with me."

They walked out of the lager and up a hill. My father and the boy walked up the hill unnoticed. The Lithuanians and Germans arrested everybody in the camp.

And only they two escaped, only they two.

Now, when mother came to Kiena she didn't know it was the day of liquidation, but she did hear stories that something was not right in Kiena. So mother decided to leave us in ghetto and go to Kiena with Abrasha and the German soldier. She stopped in front of my aunt's house. The husband of the Polish family, who had rented from my aunt, took out a gun and was going to kill my mother. The German soldier who was with Abrasha took out his gun and he shot in the air. The husband immediately put his gun away.

They drove on to the end of the village and learned that all the Jews were taken to Wiliciany to be put in a concentration camp. The Kiena lager was deserted. So they turned and drove to Wiliciany. It was a farmer's road, they couldn't drive too fast. My father and the little boy that was with him saw the truck and tried to hide. They were on a plain, straight, flat field. As the truck passed by, my father and the little boy had no good place to hide. My mother recognized my father. She stopped the truck. They took my father and the little boy and came back to Vilna, to ghetto.

That was just after Rosh Hashanah, two days before Yom Kippur. I remember when my father arrived home, he said, "Today in my heart it is

Simchas Torah, the celebration of receiving the Torah, not *erev Yom Kippur*, the solemn Day of Judgment." He had no place to hide along the road, and that's how he came back to the ghetto. Otherwise my mother would have gone on to Wiliciany.

Later, we found out there was no concentration camp there in Wiliciany. That's how we lost all of our family in Kiena. The Germans shot over three thousand Jews.

After the war, at a survivors' reunion in Israel, a young man, a stranger, came up to me and asked, "Are you Hirshka Varshavtchik?" I looked at him and did not know him. He said, "I'm Solkah Defishikah's son. Your father took me out from Kiena." I hugged him and cried.

Chapter 4: Finding the Russian Army

The next day, in October of 1941, the day before Yom Kippur, I left the house. I said goodbye to my father, to my mother, and I left the house. I said, "I'll walk, I'll go toward Minsk."

I knew that Minsk was very bad because Lolkah told us about Minsk, about the lager—600,000 to a million people. And they were shooting two hundred people every day, like nothing. I felt that the gentiles were killing innocent people just because they were Jewish. I said, "If I have to die, I might as well die fighting, but I'm not going to die without a fight." I would leave in hopes of joining an army.

Another reason why I thought to leave was I wanted to make it easier for my family for food and for documents. A set of documents, a yellow sign, for people who lived in the ghetto was a lot of money to buy. The yellow sign was your papers. You had to have it with you at all times. The papers stated that you were a specialist, that you worked. Let's say, you were a printer, or a painter, or a cabinetmaker. Having the papers allowed you work.

For food we had coupons and got so much food. With one less mouth to feed the food would go a little further. So I said, "When I leave, it will be more money for you." I didn't take one cent from the house, not one penny.

And certainly, my mother cried, and my father cried, and they wished me good luck, and said we'll see what the future will be. And this is when I went to the east.

Every day went out columns of workers to work in the morning, and they were coming back at night. But with me it was different. When I went out from the ghetto to go to look for a better future or whatever, it was like five o'clock in the evening, six o'clock in the evening erev Yom Kippur. Everybody was back home already.

I walked out of the ghetto; the Jewish policeman let me through. We knew each other. He was also from Beitar. He let me out and I went with the sidewalk, which was not allowed. The Jews had to walk in the gutter outside the ghetto. By the main gate were at least, fifteen Lithuanian policemen and about thirty German officers. Now why would there be so many officers? I didn't find out until later what was planned for that night. One Lithuanian policeman walked over to me and said, "Where are you going?"

"Across the street to the drugstore," I told him. "My father is sick and I need medicine." Jews were not allowed in the drugstore. They others didn't know what we were talking about and they let me go. Just like this, I swear to G-d. I said my father was very sick and I needed medicine, and on the next corner was a big drugstore. I kept walking. It's at least, from where he stopped me to the drugstore, maybe three hundred feet up the hill. But then I passed the store by and walked up the hill and away from the ghetto. I took off the Jewish star and walked away.

Only later on, after I returned to the ghetto, did I find out what happened that very night. Yechial told me the Nazis surrounded the ghetto. They were looking only for the men with the yellow sign, the yellow document. My family was allowed to leave the ghetto. Men with the yellow document were allowed to take their families – his wife and children up to twelve years old. The Nazis let the families out from the ghetto and let them go to the father's *ainheight*, to his place of work outside the ghetto.

After letting everybody out, then they came into the ghetto and took away—let's see—I don't remember now how many, but at least six thousand people. They brought them all to Ponary. The Nazis took children, even young people, and certainly the elderly. First of all, nobody knew exactly what was Ponary. Nobody could imagine that they were taking the people to shoot them. It made no logic. And even when we knew, we didn't want to believe it.

If someone told us that he knew about Ponary, we thought he was looking to make a name for himself. But we didn't believe it 'til—eh, I guess in March of '42, something like this. This was when the Nazis start bringing in people from the little ghettos outside Vilna. They were taking the people, and instead of dropping them off in the ghetto, they took them by train to Ponary and that's it...nobody came back from there, nobody but one that I knew.

Laika Wopnick, Moshe's wife, had a nephew who survived the war and he lived in Israel. He came back from the war with a bullet in his head. He came back with a bullet in him; the doctors couldn't take it out and that is how he lived the rest of his life 'til he died of natural causes in Israel. He received the bullet in his head at Ponary. He told me that after he was shot and fell into a pit, dead bodies fell on top of him. So many people just died lying there because they couldn't get out, couldn't climb over the dead. They were covered with bodies and couldn't get out. He managed to climb over the dead bodies and get out.

When my father walked out with my mother and Yechial, Yechial was the only child that he had with him. I don't know where Lolkah was, but he was not with them. My father had papers for three children though, so he took three children. He took Rivka Adlofka. She was nine years old. She was holding my father's hand. The second girl was Shames from Zavel's *shul*, temple. She was Zavel's youngest daughter. We were all neighbors in the same courtyard. Shames was two years younger than Yechial. My father was holding hands with his "daughters" and Yechial was on the other side of them. A German, or a Lithuanian, grabbed Yechial—who was on the outside of the family line—by the hand and tried to pull him out to the left, to the Ponary line.

My father felt at that time, when they grabbed Yechial, that he would die; that maybe he did a mistake by taking the two other children. Yechial tried to pull out of the soldier's grip. Yechial pulled back and my father shouted, and somehow, at the last second, the soldier let him go and this was how Yechial survived that night. This I didn't find out until I returned to the ghetto.

I walked for two weeks, mostly at night. I walked one hundred and twenty kilometers. I slept during the daytime in the woods. I ate raw potatoes from farmers' fields, and drank from streams. At night I would knock on a door and ask a farmer for a piece of bread. Most of the time I had to steal food, I couldn't ask. I was wearing a Lithuanian soldier's shirt, which I stole from one of the farmers. I still remember the metal buttons. I wore that shirt for a long time.

Once I knocked on the door of a Polish home and a woman gave me a slice of bread, about a pound, a pound slice. She cut off a piece of solid bacon, then said, "You are Jewish, you don't eat bacon," so she gave me a piece of cheese instead. Some people were kind, and some people said, "Run away because I'm going to kill you."

After two weeks of walking, I was so tired I lay down behind a tree and slept. I was awakened and saw maybe one hundred soldiers around me. I was so happy. They talked to me in Russian, but my Russian was so poor they became suspicious.

"From where are you coming, what are you doing, who are you?"

And I told them, "I ran away from the ghetto and I'm going East, I'm going to Russia."

One soldier said, "He sounds like a German. I think he is a spy."

I had a piece of bread in my pants and said, "This is what I eat and this is all I have."

They took me, and they grabbed me and searched me. They brought a wagon with a horse, and they made me get up on the wagon. They threw a rope over a tree and I said, "What? Are you crazy?"

And they tied my hands and they put a rope around my neck. I looked at them from one to another. The rope was tight, burning my neck. They were counting, getting ready to hit the horse, to make him gallop. Then I recognized someone, I recognized someone! "Tavarish Natchalnik Piekarnia Voyentorga, come help me! Tavarish Natchalnik! Tavarish Natchalnik!"

Tavarish Natchalnik was on horseback. He rushed over to the crowd. "Immediately, right away. Release him, immediately! I know this boy." Tavarish Natchalnik, the Russian captain who had taught me to drive, cut the rope off my neck. He vouched for me and took me into the Russian army.

I saw Tavarish Natchalnik Piekarnia Voyentorga again only one other time. I don't know whatever happened to him. Tavarish Natchalnik Piekarnia Voyentorga saved my life.

I was put in a group with a machine gunner. I was number three in the group. There is a *pulimiochik*, the number one, with the machine gun. I don't remember the *pulimiochik's* name, only that he was from Odessa. Then there is the number two, who carries the extra bullets. And I was number three, I watched the number two. I carried two big disks of bullets for the machine gun. My job was to watch the number two, to help him help the *pulimiochik*. The number two's name was Kolka. Wherever the machine gun went, it was my job to follow. Kolka and I became like brothers. He would never take a bite without me, and I would never take a bite without him. The number one had plenty to drink; vodka, plenty of vodka. Kolka and I were stinkers, not drinkers.

Usually our job as the machine gun group was to either be in front to protect the group or to be in the rear. A week or two after I joined the army, there were two Germans on bicycles who were riding toward us. We let them get very close then opened fire. The number one machine gunner, the *pulimiochik*, killed them both. We were so anxious to get to the Germans that I rushed and pulled off the boots from one of them and took a rifle. I was treated like a hero even though it wasn't my doing, it was the *pulimiochik*. I had had a pair of shoes that weren't worth five cents. I had to tie them up with a piece of string; otherwise, they would fall off my feet. I wore the boots for a long time. Those boots really helped me. They were rubberized leather. It was a really cold winter that year.

We patrolled in the swamps of White Russia. We learned about blowing up trains from the people who did it, because we used to prepare the dynamite before going to the train. For example, the one who carried the dynamite never carried the *polnik*, the fuse. And the one who carried the fuse, stayed far away from the guy that carried the dynamite.

Whether we were in a group of fifty or one hundred, Kolka and I only stayed with the machine gunner. We did whatever he told us to do. We didn't know what missions we were going on or what we might find when we got there. We only stayed with him.

Everyone carried a wooden spoon in their boot. Without it you couldn't eat. We had two meals a day. We had a field kitchen. For breakfast we ate from a big pot of kasha, mixed grains. For dinner we ate whatever meat that could be taken from a local farmer. When we were on the road I was never allowed to leave the machine gun to go to a house to grab a piece of bread. If the *pulimiochik* went into a house for bread, we could follow him, because we followed him everywhere.

I stayed with the Russians for three and a half months; October, November, December, and part of January. I never shaved. I never took a haircut for three and a half months.

I think it was the beginning of 1942, in January, or maybe even February; the whole area became surrounded by the Germans. They didn't stop bombing us, not for one night. I don't think the bombs did as much damage as the branches from the trees. The splintering wood killed so many of us unexpectedly. Kolka and I didn't know where to go. The number one, the *pulimiochik*, had been killed. He lay dead in the snow. An exploding branch went in from his back, up out his front. Thankfully, he died instantly. It was not like when you get hurt and you suffer and you bleed a lot, he died instantly.

There were fifteen thousand of us when the Russian commander gave the order, "*Kto-Kuda.*" The order was Kto-Kuda. Kto-Kuda. Disband. Go wherever you want. Wherever you can go. Just come back after the blockade. That day, after the order to Kto-Kuda, Kolka and I started to walk to the west. I said to Kolka, "We'll go to Vilna. This is what I know, so we'll try to survive."

It started snowing and it started to get dark. We had a *kazuch*, a long fur coat. The coat reached down to my ankles. We decided to lie down underneath it to stay warm. We fell asleep. What woke us up were voices, German voices.

Underneath the fur coat we took out the safety pin from a grenade and we agreed, "If we get caught, we're not going away. We'll just let it go and that's all to it."

We lay there for at least five hours, waiting, listening. Finally, after hours of silence, we got up. We saw the tracks of the soldiers who had come within three feet of the kazuch. They had passed on either side of us. It wasn't brains that saved us; it was *mazel*, grace and good fortune. Mazel is often translated as luck. It means much more than that. It is from the same root as the stars. Mazel is what we bring with us, what is in our nature, when we are born, what we have brought with us from the stars.

I didn't want to go back to Vilna, but had no choice. We didn't know where else to go so we headed west. Kolka had an automatic rifle, a *pehpershar* it's called, with one disk and two sleeves of bullets. We walked for five days. It was winter, a blizzard. Cold; maybe thirty-five degrees below zero; wind, fifty miles per hour. The snow was swirling. We came to a village called Larvarischk.

In this village I recognized the house of an aunt of mine, my father's oldest sister. We saw a little light in her house. We walked toward the light. It seemed to take forever, but at last we came to her house. It was very long, maybe one hundred fifty feet long with the barn. It was like a motel for the farmers who traveled with a sled. They could sleep the night and keep away from the cold.

We walked through the part of the shed for the animals, then went into the house. It was very dark. The only light was from a *luchinka*, a one fourth of an inch thick strip of wood, lit at one end and pointed at the other. It took about fifteen minutes for one to burn. Before it ended, someone lit another one and stuck it back into a notch in the wall.

One luchinka was the only light in a big room. There were, I don't remember, one or two farmers, and a woman sitting at the end of a table. She said to me,

"*To Zyd.*" It meant, this is a Jew. This she said like she would spit on me. Kolka pulled out the gun and wanted to kill her right on the spot.

We tied her up, we didn't kill her. I swear we didn't kill her. We tied up the farmers, very nice and quiet. We took away one wagon with wood. Food we took from the sleds. They had two or three loaves of bread, chicken, bacon and cheese, and butter. From there, that very night, with a horse and wagon we headed out for Vilna. Nobody stopped us, not soldiers or even police. We were driving like farmers going to the market.

Chapter 5: Life in the Vilna Ghetto

We traveled that night—seven hours, maybe—and came into Vilna ghetto late in the afternoon of the next day. Kolka stayed by a Polish family not far from the ghetto. This was a gentile family that I knew. We gave the family a big loaf of bread, maybe eight kilo, ten kilo; a big loaf. This they enjoyed.

I told them I had to go to the ghetto to see my parents. We were two or three blocks from the ghetto. When groups of people were returning to ghetto from work I came to the gate and said, "I'm Varshavtchik's son. I want to go into the ghetto."

A group of workers grabbed me. They took off the big kazuch, the long coat, and put on a different coat on me. The workers knew that the kazuch was not a coat for people in the ghetto. It was a farmer's coat, a gentile's coat, and they didn't want me to stand out.

I came into the house and certainly my mother was crying. My father wasn't home yet; he was at work. Lolkah wasn't home. Neither was Abrasha. They came later. The only ones I saw in the house—that I remember in the house—were my mother and her sister Rikle.

When it came time to go to eat dinner, I had to go to the bathroom. The bathroom was outside like in a little hill. On the way back from the bathroom, the commandant from the Jewish police of the ghetto said, "I see your face for the first time in ghetto. I have to find out from where you are and who you are."

He arrested me.

My father came home. Lolkah came home. Abrasha came home. It was time for dinner, but I was not there. Where did I go? They went to the toilet and couldn't find me. So my father went to the police and found me there. "This is my son."

"Yeah, but Muszkat arrested him."

So my father said, "Okay. He won't run away. If you need him, he'll come and talk to you." I was released into my father's custody.

I had such a bad feeling already about the ghetto that I was ready to go back to the jungle, regardless of what they told me. Sure enough, one of the policemen in the precinct who must have been a member of the FPO, the Fareynikte Partizaner Organizatsye (United Partisan Organization) came to talk to me. I told him, "I don't belong here. I'm going back to the army. The order was 'Kto-Kuda', and that's how I came here, but I have to go back."

Word got out that a partisan was in the ghetto. This time I was arrested by the chief of police, Joseph Glazman. My father was there in the house, and he said, "I must go with him. I won't let you take him like this. I want to know what the charges are." They agreed and brought me to Yunden Rat, the main office of the Jewish Community, the city hall.

Around the table were twenty people sitting. At the head of the table was Joseph Glazman who was the chief of the police from the ghetto. He said, "Don't be afraid. Just tell me from where you've come, what you did, how's the life there. Tell me everything that's happened to you."

And I was afraid. I said, "I don't know anything. I was hiding by gentiles. I don't even know their names."

There was a brother of a friend of mine, Kover was his name. He said, "Do you know me? Will you trust me? Will you tell your story to me?"

I said, "I can't tell you anything. I have to have my father guarantee to me that I can tell you the story. Then I'll tell you."

As well as my father, they brought a rabbi, Rabbi Freid. Rabbi Freid guaranteed that everything I would tell them is off the record. Nobody will know about it. And that I'm secured. They gave a guarantee to my father that nothing would happen to me, that everything I told them would be secret and that they were there only to help me, not to hurt me.

After I received a guarantee, I started to tell them my story. Four people were present. Joseph Glazman, and Sonya Madayska were from the *Tzecka* Party, the Communist Party, but I didn't know their names at that time. I also didn't know that Joseph Glazman was one of the organizers of the FPO—the *Fareynikte Partizaner Organizatsye*—the United Partisan Organization. This was the *shtab*, headquarters, of the FPO, but this I didn't know either. Joseph Glazman was also a Beitar before the war, a member of Bet Trumpledor, like me, but this too I didn't know at the time. Abba Kovner was present too. He was another founder of the FPO. He was a member of Shomer Ha'tzair. They were the political group who wanted to negotiate with the Arabs to establish the state of Israel. Borka Friedman was the fourth person there. He was the head of the Beitar in Vilna.

The leaders started telling me that Germans are killing Jews, sending them out to Ponary, killing and burying them, and they want to save as much prestige for the Jewish people in the Vilna ghetto as possible. Some said we should put up a defense in the ghetto, and some said we should send people out to the woods to become the *partisana* and fight the Germans in a jungle-type fight.-

They were Jewish fighters. There were no Jewish partisans yet—they were just Jewish fighters. Partisans meant they were in the woods. Fighters meant they could be anyplace.

The leaders were trying to organize a movement in the ghetto to save as much Jewish youth as possible. That was why they wanted to hear from me what was going on with the Russian partisans. And I told them, "It's not a partisan group, it's a regular army." To me it was a regular army because most of them, 95%, were in uniform—Russian uniform.

Anyway, I told them I had a friend. I told them where he was waiting for me outside the ghetto with a wagon and horse that didn't belong to us, that we had taken away. I told them I have the kazuch that was Kolka's and mine. I told them, "I have to bring it to him and I have to see him. I have to know what is going to happen." I told them my story. I told them what happened to me.

Joseph Glazman told me first what they could do for me: they would make me a policeman. I laughed in their faces. They would make me a policeman, but with special authority. "There are two like this in the ghetto. You will have a document which says you're allowed to go by yourself any place in the city. You can go in any office outside the ghetto where Jewish people are working." They told me I would be able to go by myself, have one person with me, or fifty people with me. I could take them any place as long as it is to work or from work. They also told me the Germans were going to open up a new railroad line, and that I'd be able to take workers from the ghetto by train as far as thirty kilometers outside of Vilna and bring them back.

The Germans trusted the Jewish police very much. They trusted the police as if the police were Gestapo. They had their reasons. Anything they wanted to do, they talked to the Chief of Police in the ghetto, Joseph Glazman, and his word was just like—how should I tell it—like the law. He said something and that was the law. No questions asked.

The Jewish police could even hang people in the ghetto, not because the Germans asked them to, but because those people had broken the law. But the police called in the Germans, they should witness it.

At that time Joseph Glazman was the Chief of the Police. He was secretly doing things the Germans didn't want to happen. Not every Jewish policeman knew this, not every policeman was involved. Joseph Glazman had big problems. Sometimes he had to go along with a German decision that wasn't good for the Jews, like taking away the children, or like taking away the disabled, but the Germans would have done it anyway.

The next morning, three Jewish police escorted me out of the ghetto. We had no trouble leaving. Kolka and I had breakfast together. I returned the kazuch to him. I told him I had no use for it in the ghetto. Only then did he take it. We were led to an alley behind a church. There were standing two guards. They blindfolded us, and took us into the house, in front of a committee from the Communist Polish Central Party.

I was blindfolded all the time. They asked me questions, and they asked Kolka questions. When I came to the meeting I was in boots, the boots I got from a dead soldier. I told them how it was in Russia, what we were doing, how they organized food, how sometimes we went away from the base for five or six days, but at least everybody had a loaf of bread. I even told them that everybody had a big spoon; you needed a spoon because no one could take from the pot with their hands.

We were interviewed from early in the morning until late at night. That night we slept there. The next morning they took me back to the ghetto; Kolka remained with them. They would notify the Soviet authorities that he and I were not deserters, and that we were alive.

I did not see Kolka anymore. They just told me that Kolka would remain with them. I never found out what happened to him. Kolka had a heart of gold, a heart of gold.

They would take care of the wagon with the wood; they would bring it to a marketplace, tie up the horse, and let him stay. They would send me back to the ghetto. I should see the representative of the Tzecka Party, Sonya Madayska.

They returned me to the ghetto with a group of people returning from work. And when I came to the ghetto, there was already a yellow paper left for me. This was the legal document that allowed me to be in the ghetto. Wives had pink papers. You had to have it with you all the time. When they stopped you on the street, in ghetto, or outside of ghetto, you had to have it. That was your document.

I was told I should go to the office of Joseph Glazman and pick up my paper. I went to the office; the paper was ready for me. There was a pink paper for a wife, without a name. It was put in the safe; whenever I needed it, if I needed it, it would be ready. Joseph Glazman had a certificate made in German and Lithuanian stating I was allowed to go into any German establishment where Jewish people are working to check on their working conditions. I was allowed to travel alone, or in a small or large group outside the ghetto. What I didn't know at the time, but would later find out is the reason for my papers. My documents would allow me to move around the city and smuggle in what I could to the ghetto. Joseph Glazman introduced me to the FPO.

They gave me an order that I shouldn't talk to anybody. Nobody should know from where I came, or what I saw. I should walk clean-shaven, not with a beard. Someone gave me a haircut. They took me to the showers.

My family didn't know what happened while I was with the Russian army. When I returned, Lolkah asked me. Very little I told him. I was not allowed to tell, because it was like a military secret. He didn't insist. Just like we never knew much of what happened to him while he was in the Minsk camp. They'd tried to hang Lolkah in Minsk. Lolkah didn't tell me though. Somebody else who was with him did—one of the other five who came back with him. It was one of the things he didn't like to talk about. It was a painful thing for him, and we didn't insist he should tell us.

My family lived in a tiny apartment in the ghetto. We had two rooms and a little kitchen. The kitchen was small but there was little cooking to do. My parents were eating only kosher. They would walk around for days with only a *sthickel*, a piece, of bread. If there was a piece of chicken, it wasn't kosher, so they wouldn't touch it. Everyone except for Lolkah and me ate where they worked. Rikle ate where her sister Itke worked. There was not much food in the house and not much cooking. There was just enough food to survive.

In the one room that we had, on the floor on bricks, we had one long couch from one end of the room to the other. We made it into one long bed. There were the three children laying there with seven adults. In the other room was another family of ten. During the day all of us were out working, all except my mother. Our house was so clean that you could eat off the floor. When a German inspector came into the ghetto to check for the cleanliness of the apartments, our apartment was the one shown to him. Once I remember I was sitting in the doorway. There was a sack with flour on the floor standing and they brought in a German inspector. He pointed with his finger, "What is this?"

I said right away, "This is for the whole building. *A mont proveana*. This is food for the whole month, for the building."

He didn't question any more.

For a short period of time there was a theatre in the ghetto. There was a coffee house. There was a school. The whole time there was a ghetto there was the *Judenrat*, the Jewish government.

Refugees were sometimes brought into the ghetto. They were taken from smaller nearby ghettos and brought here. Other small ghettos were closed and all those Jews were taken to Ponary to be killed.

As a Jewish policeman and as a holder of the document that I could take people to work, they gave me a job to take people to work on the railroad to a town which is about, I would say, 30 kilometers away from Vilna. It was called *Naye Vileyke*, the New Vilna. We left the ghetto about six o'clock every morning. I walked with the workers to the station. There we had prepared for us two or three cars. The train took us to Naye Vileyke.

My job was just for safety. I had to make sure the workers were protected. I also was responsible that they should do their jobs, and that they shouldn't run away. There was also a foreman, Warhaftik was his name. He and his wife, a young boy and his wife, they kept account of the names because the workers got paid every day. If they worked on Monday, they used to get paid on Tuesday. If they worked Saturday, they used to get paid on Sunday, seven days a week. After a days' work, Warhaftik turned in the papers to the railroad supervisor, who brought the payroll the next day.

I came with a hundred people to work, and went back with maybe eighty. I used to "lose" them; the workers tried to trade with gentiles for food. Workers brought extra clothes. For a shirt for example, they could get two loaves of bread. So it never happened that I took the same amount of people back to the ghetto. But it also happened that the next day, I went with eighty workers and I left with ninety, because ten people showed up from the day before.

Nobody tried to escape. Where were they going to run? This was a little town with a big railroad station. There was no place to run to. Workers went to gentiles and tried to trade whatever they had with them for food. They stayed the night, and then in the morning, came back to work. Sometimes Molly Kiejdan—she was one of those workers who slept overnight outside to trade with the villagers—she was in the group. I didn't know her at the time. Fanya knew her though. Molly's husband, Pinchus, had been in her class. He used to sit behind her and dip her braids into the inkwell.

Afterwards, the workers returned to ghetto. I never reported my count was wrong.

Once it happened that the Germans held us up. The Gestapo came and assembled everybody on the railroad track. They counted and asked me how many men I had. I had to think fast. I told them I didn't know. I didn't have my papers with me and I couldn't give the exact count. I left the papers in the railroad office, and it was closed already.

The Germans surrounded us, but I walked amongst the Jewish workers speaking to them in Yiddish, "Make believe I am the worst bastard in the world. Stay on your knees and beg me. Make believe you're more afraid of me than the Germans." Out loud, in German, I cursed at them and told them, "Wait till we get back to the ghetto, just wait!"

And that's what they did, yeah. The Germans believed the workers were more afraid of me than the Gestapo.

In the meantime, the train left and we were still at the railroad station. I counted the number of us to myself so when the Gestapo came again I should know the exact count. But what happened was they brought in two workers who were caught in the village trying to trade.

When I saw the Germans were going to arrest them, I came over to the workers and slapped their faces. I cursed at them. I didn't let the Germans take them away. I told the Germans, "I'm taking these two to ghetto chief. The chief of police will take care of them. They'll get punished for it."

Maybe I saved their lives. Who knows… maybe all our lives.

After I got the workers away from the Germans, we rode another train to the railroad station, arriving at ten o'clock that night. From the station to the ghetto was about, I would say, six or seven blocks. I put them up in fours and we marched like soldiers. We arrived at the ghetto after ten o'clock, long after curfew, but at least we brought everybody. We didn't lose a single worker.

Just inside the ghetto gates were the Jewish police. On the outside were the Lithuanian police. But we marched so fast that both sides opened up the gates completely and we just walked in. That was it. The next day, instead of having one hundred twenty people reporting for work, I only had maybe seventy.

Pasha Derewianski was my contact in the FPO, the Fareynikte Partizaner Organizatsye (United Partisan Organization). She would come to my house as my girl friend. We would go out on a date and she would give me all the notes and all the orders. She would tell there was a meeting at a certain time in a certain place and I would go.

We had different kinds of meetings. First of all, we taught the people how to take apart a gun and how to put it together. They had to do it blindfolded. Blindfolded! They had to take it apart, all the pieces, and then blindfolded, put it together. At the meetings, we also told what we heard on the radio from England. At the end of every meeting, we sang The Partisan's Hymn, *"Zog Nit Keyn Mol."* Never Say You're Going on Your Last Road. This song was written by Hirsh Glick, a partisan, a poet. He was shot after escaping from a Nazi camp in Estonia.

The meetings were in small groups; five, plus the instructor, who came with a gun. Tops, seven, but mostly only five. This was done that you shouldn't know who else belonged to the FPO.

I knew more than five because I was the instructor for more than one group. I met with a group at least once a week. I taught people the safety of the gun, like, "Never point the gun with your finger on the trigger, period. Never, never hold the gun with the bullets in it. First you take out the magazine with the bullets, and then you check if there is another bullet besides in the barrel."

The less anybody knew, the better—for them and for me. For example, I never told what happened with workers in *Naye Vileyke,* the New Vilna. I never came to a meeting and told how many guns I smuggled into the ghetto. The less anybody knew the better.

זאָג ניט קיין מאָל
ZOG NIT KEYN MOL
(Never Say)

זאָג ניט קיין מאָל, אַז דו גייסט דעם לעצטן וועג,
כאָטש הימלען בלײַענע פֿאַרשטעלן בלויע טעג, —
קומען וועט נאָך אונדזער אויסגעבענקטע שעה,
ס'וועט אַ פּויק טאָן אונדזער טראָט — מיר זײַנען דאָ!

פֿון גרינעם פּאַלמענלאַנד ביז ווײַסן לאַנד פֿון שניי
מיר קומען אָן מיט אונדזער פּײַן, מיט אונדזער וויי,
און וווּ געפֿאַלן איז אַ שפּריץ פֿון אונדזער בלוט,
שפּראָצן וועט דאָרט אונדזער גבֿורה, אונדזער מוט!

ס'וועט די מאָרגנזון באַגילדן אונדז דעם הײַנט,
און דער נעכטן וועט פֿאַרשווינדן מיטן פֿײַנט;
נאָר אויב פֿאַרזאַמען וועט די זון און דער קאַיאָר,
ווי אַ פּאַראָל וועט גיין דאָס ליד פֿון דור צו דור!

דאָס ליד געשריבן איז מיט בלוט און ניט מיט בלײַ,
ס'איז ניט קיין לידל פֿון אַ פֿויגל אויף דער פֿרײַ, —
דאָס האָט אַ פֿאָלק צווישן פֿאַלנדיקע ווענט
דאָס ליד געזונגען מיט נאַגאַנעס' אין די הענט!...

Zog Nit Keyn Mol - Never Say

Never say that there is only death for you,
Though leaden skies may be concealing days of blue—
Because the hour that we have hungered for is near;
Beneath our tread the earth shall tremble: We are here!

From land of palm-tree to the far-off land of snow
We shall be coming with our torment and our woe,
And everywhere our blood has sunk into the earth
Shall our bravery, our vigor blossom forth!

We'll have the morning sun to set our days aglow,
And all our yesterdays shall vanish with the foe,
And if the time is long before the sun appears,
Then let this song go like a signal through the years.

This song was written with our blood and not with lead;
It's not a song that birds sing overhead.
It was a people, among toppling barricades,
That sang this song of ours with pistols and grenades.

Never say that there is only death for you,
Though leaden skies may be concealing days of blue -
Because the hour that we have hungered for is near;
Beneath our tread the earth shall tremble: We are here!
Translated into English by Aaron Kremer

The FPO had a radio. We received news from London. Very few people knew about this, the less the better. This was how we kept up with news about the war. At the places of work where the Germans were, you could see on the faces of the soldiers how the war was going. When the war was going well for us you could sometimes see a red army star under the soldiers' hats if they were worried about being caught by the Russians. That way they could say they were supporting the Russians.

Another job I had was to go to the railroad station to meet a man; his name was Fifke di Pomele. Fifke di Pomele was fumigating the bugs in the railroad cars. They called him Fifke di Pomele because before the war he was a pickpocket, a thief. But the moment he came into the ghetto, he came to the authorities and he said, "I'm a thief, but from now on, I'll never steal a penny that doesn't belong to me from anybody in the ghetto."

I used to go to Fifke and talk to him. I would arrange the date and time to come and pick him up from the railroad. Fifke di Pomele wore a gas mask over his face, and he came with a smoky spray to exterminate. While he did this, all the soldiers and officers, everybody, had to leave the train cars. The soldiers often left their weapons on the seats. When he could, Fifke stole a handgun, or bullets, whatever was left behind.

Besides being an exterminator, Fifke di Pomele also worked as a glazier fixing windows. He carried the glass in a toolbox that had a large hidden pocket, large enough to put in twenty pounds of potatoes. So, in this pocket underneath the glass, that was where he put in the guns. I used to escort him to the ghetto. Sometimes, I even took him into the first police precinct where I had a little office. I took out the guns and reported to my commander that I had so many guns.

We brought five, or maybe six, guns at a time. Sometimes there were none. Sometimes there were only bullets. The problem was there were different caliber handguns. Some only had the bullets that were in the gun and that was it. The Germans used a very small caliber bullet. The Belgian guns had big bullets. We smuggled in guns once or twice a week.

Sometimes, we bought guns, but whatever Fifke di Pomele gave to me, that was free. From the gentile where Kolka had stayed when he was waiting outside the ghetto, from this gentile once I bought a gun. He had purchased it from a Lithuanian. On different occasions, in different ways, we smuggled in guns as best we could, to add to the FPO's supplies.

Once, on the way back into the ghetto, on the outskirts of the city, I was stopped by two soldiers, a German and a Lithuanian. I had three guns on me; two were tucked into the waist of my pants in front and the third was tucked in at my back. I showed the German my papers and he saluted me, saying, "Go." The Lithuanian said, *"Palalk!"* Wait!

When he said to wait, my face turned white, not because of me, but because of my family. The guns I have by my stomach have no trigger. I know I can't shoot him. The two soldiers started fighting between themselves whether I should be searched or not.

The German got so mad that he pulled his rifle on the Lithuanian. He had seen my documents. It was written in German, had the Gestapo seal, including the proper signatures, from the Arbeitsabteilung, the Labor Department, from City Hall, even from the Lithuanian police.

I was shaking. All I could think about was they were going to kill my family. The Germans would kill everyone in the ghetto with the name Varshavtchik.

Sometimes the Germans would kill everyone in the entire apartment building if someone was found out.

Finally, the Lithuanian soldier let the German soldier have his way. I hurried past them and saw a place where Jewish workers were. Most everyone from the ghetto knew me because I was a police officer. It was a German courthouse. I went inside to catch my breath.

One worker said to me, "*Ikh hob fuftsik kilo mel.* I have fifty kilos flour. Can you take me to the ghetto?"

I was happy to have someone to walk with. I took two men. They were carrying the flour underneath their coats. Each man had a sack on one side and a sack on the other side with straps over the shoulders. On top of the flour they put on a coat. If they would be searched, they certainly would be found out. So that's when they said to me, "*Hirshka, nem undz arayn in ghetto. Gib glakh tsu dayn tatin di mel.*" Take us into the ghetto. Right away we will give the flour to your father.

I was relieved to lead them. You get shot whether the guns are broken or not. You get the same bullet if it's a gun or if it's flour. We knew one woman whose sister was caught with a kilo of *arbes*, peas. She was caught by the head of the Gestapo himself. Not Ganz, not Dessler, no Jewish officials could talk the Germans out of it—they wouldn't change their minds—they should let her live. Officials tried to bail her out with gold and still the Gestapo refused. She was taken to Ponary.

I used to bring the guns to the Peneusov brothers. They checked them out and wrote down the serial number of each one. I don't know what they needed it for, but anyway the brothers had a record of those guns by the serial number.

Then, in the next day or two, I went to the Peneusov brothers, took away the guns, and brought them to my house. We lived on Szpitalna Street, #11. Across the street from my house was a building with a basement. Nobody lived there. The entrance to that building was on Szpitalna Street, # 9, the next courtyard. But from #11, you could walk into the basement of #9. There were no windows on this side, only the entrance to the basement.

Fanya's father, Zalman Raichel, was the one who built me two hiding places with two big boxes. He was an artist and a sculptor. Without knowing where to look you could not see that there was a hiding place at all. He didn't know for what reason he made these hiding places. What would be going into the boxes, he didn't know, and he didn't ask. That's where I kept the guns.

Fifke di Pomele wasn't a member of the FPO. He didn't know where the guns were going. He knew the guns were going for the partisans, for underground work, but he didn't know names or anything. We did this at least thirty or forty times. All in all, we smuggled in over two hundred guns.

My parents never knew what I was doing. I couldn't involve them. It was safer for all of us.

Once, I think it was in 1942; two partisans came to the ghetto and were arrested. Joseph Glazman wasn't the chief of the ghetto police anymore. The Gestapo no longer trusted Glazman and had replaced him with Ganz. Ganz was also Jewish and was a captain in the Lithuanian army. Ganz was in charge of the *Judenrat*, the Jewish government. Joseph Glazman and Ganz did not get along. Ganz didn't want the young Jews to join the partisans. Perhaps he thought that he would be able to fight his way out of the ghetto. Or maybe, he was afraid that if escaping Jews were caught the Germans would liquidate the ghetto. Dessler was chosen by the Gestapo as assistant to Ganz. Dessler became the chief of the ghetto police. Before the war Dessler was a good friend of my father's. But being chief of police changed him. You couldn't talk to him anymore.

I don't know how or why, but Ganz was afraid to turn the arrested partisans over to the Gestapo. He was afraid to start up with the FPO, the Fareynikte Partizaner Organizatsye (United Partisan Organization). He was afraid what would happen in the ghetto if the Gestapo killed the two partisans. He thought there would be fighting in the ghetto between the Jewish police that he oversaw and the FPO. Somehow, Ganz managed to turn them over to Joseph Glazman who was now second in command of the FPO. From these two partisans we, in the FPO, found out the movement of the partisans, what they were doing, and how near they were to us in the Vilna ghetto. Now, for the first time, we had a place to go.

Jewish laborers went to work outside the ghetto. Some groups were sent to the woods to cut lumber for the Germans in Vilna. It was a very hard winter. The Germans needed the wood to burn for heat. The laborers came back and told stories about partisans. Molly Kiejdan was in a group of workers who cut wood at night. The watchman, the German soldier, gave her his rifle in case partisans came, it would appear that he was her prisoner.

My job for the Labor Department, leading workers out of the ghetto gave me the opportunity to take out groups from the FPO, take them from the ghetto. Borka Friedman was in the first group, the Beitar group. Freid, also from Beitar, was a captain from the police in the ghetto. He came with his daughter, and then there was one, the *keymenkerer*, chimney sweep. In all there were about thirty people. I led them twenty-five kilometers south by southwest from Vilna to a gentile named Tatar Villikan who lived on the outskirts of the jungle. He was a big, strong man, about 6' 4". Villikan, who had no liking for the Germans, was paid by the FPO to lead the groups I brought to him into the Rudnik Jungle.

After taking this group to Villikan, I didn't see anyone from the group again during the war. I did meet a few who'd survived after the war, later, in Israel.

I led people into the woods many times. At this time, taking people out was organized maybe once a month, once in two months. The FPO organized the escape; extra clothes, weapons, all hidden. Twenty people or so escaped at a time. Fifteen guns were held in two bundles. Two of the twenty guarded those bundles with their lives. Sometimes they met before the gate and I took them by train together with the workers to New Vilna. That was the easiest way.

During the day those twenty people worked their shift, just like anyone else. This group always worked the furthest into the woods. At dusk they hid and escaped at night. I came back to the ghetto with the rest of the workers like nothing happened. Unless you were part of the group that was escaping, you knew nothing of what was going on.

Sometimes we assembled and I took the group out of town like workers going to work. I could lead larger groups because I had the documents. Documents like this were only two in the whole ghetto. I had a set and Toby, another Labor Department official, had a set. Toby was not in the FPO.

Politics had nothing to do with FPO, Fareynikte Partizaner Organizatsye (United Partisan Organization). People from Beitar, the Tzecka Party, Shomer Ha'tzair, and others all joined the FPO. In FPO was only one thing, take out as much as we could, save as much as we could, and take *nekome*, revenge, as much as we could.

We had different assignments in the police department. A captain above me would say, "You have to go there to this German *einhite*, to this German unit. Check out if they have problems with workers."

That was my job, to go and check it all out, and report back. I protected workers so they wouldn't get in trouble, so they wouldn't get arrested by the Lithuanian or the German police. Anything happens, any place, on a workplace, if a Lithuanian or a German caught one or more of the workers stealing or anything, I came. I smacked the workers' faces, arrested them, and took them back to the ghetto—and then let them go free. Anything I had to do was better than them being taken by the Lithuanian or the German police.

It was in March, on a Friday, I was sent by Ganz, the ghetto chief, to the *bahnhof*, the railroad station, to the chief of the Gestapo there, who had arrested a Jew on the railroad. Ganz thought it was a partisan. To Ganz, saving a partisan was a very big deal. Ganz wanted to protect himself. He felt that after the war, he might be arrested as a German collaborator by the Russian army, or whoever was going to liberate Vilna. If he could show that he helped the partisans, it would be to his benefit. My orders were I should go there and bring the Jew who was arrested back to ghetto.

It was Shabbos, Friday night. So I went there and I knocked on the door of the Gestapo chief. He said, "Come in."

I entered a very big hall with one desk. He was sitting behind the desk on a chair. From where I was standing to his desk was about twenty feet, a very big hall. The floor was marbled cement.

I saluted him. He said, "Come closer."

I walked the twenty feet to his desk. I saluted again and said to him, "My name is Hirshka Varshavtchik. The ghetto chief sent me here because a Jew who ran away from work was arrested. I have to bring him to ghetto for punishment and for an interview with the ghetto chief."

Slowly he stood up, walked around the desk and stood before me. With his fist he gave me a *zets*, a wallop, in the face, in my right ear. It was such a powerful zets that I fell down and slid on the marbled cement twenty feet from his desk to the doorway.

I lay there for a time. I got up and walked over to him. I saluted him again and said, "By the orders of the ghetto chief, I'm not leaving without this man who was arrested by you."

He looked at me and gave me another zets, this time in the left ear. Again

I slid from his desk to the door. I lay there on the floor. I picked myself up again.

He said to me, "I don't believe it. You're still alive? I thought you would be dead."

I didn't hear what else he said because there began a shooming in my ears. I said, "Whatever you do, I'm not going to leave without him."

He called a guard and they brought up the Jew. I don't know what else he was saying because I could hear nothing. I couldn't hear maybe for two or three hours. Blood was coming out both my ears, but I didn't know at the time.

Ganz also told me I shouldn't talk to this guy after I got him out from Gestapo, I should only bring him directly to the ghetto chief. I shouldn't let anybody talk to him. Anyway, I couldn't talk to him, because I couldn't hear anything. My ears were still ringing from the wallops.

I returned to Ganz and brought him this man. Ganz said to me I should go into the showers to wash out my ears, that it will help me. So right from there I went in *bod*, the showers, and steamed out my clothes. While I was there, I felt a little better.

My ears were clogged with blood, but I didn't pay attention to them. I went to see my commanding officer from the FPO and the Peneusov brothers to prepare for Monday. On Monday, I was supposed to go with the disinfecting truck to Swienciany. They told me that, in Swienciany, we would pick up a machine gun to hide in the disinfecting truck, and bring in to the ghetto. So I was very anxious to be healthy for Monday.

On Sunday, I had to go to the precinct. I had to be at the desk for about four or five hours. I started feeling like I was getting a cold or something. I was very shaky. I tried to put on my jacket. Another policeman came to take over the desk. I was trembling so hard I couldn't put on my jacket. One hand went in, and the other hand, I couldn't put my hand in the jacket. There was a girl, a visitor from the ghetto near the police station, I remember, she helped me put on the jacket over my shoulder and I walked home.

My father, mommy, brother Lolkah and Rikle were home. Itke wasn't there. They were playing cards or some kind of a game, I don't remember. I said, "I'm very shaky."

They said, "Okay, go lay down."

As I went to lie down I started to cough and with the cough, blood came out. Right away they ran to bring the police doctor who came in, and he said that I had pneumonia. This doctor was free for the Jewish police. Yeah, and I was with this for about three months. I remained in the house.

In fact, Ganz brought in electricity from outside the ghetto to my apartment. Nobody had electricity in the ghetto. Ganz had seen the blood dripping out of my ears and knew what had happened there, at the *bahnhof*. He brought in electrical wiring so I could be cared for in the night. He ordered for us not to let me go to the hospital, because he knew that in the middle of the night, the Gestapo came in and whoever was sick they threw them on the truck, and took them away to Ponary. The police had no control over it. So he didn't let me go to the hospital, and they treated me in the house.

But I remember I used to have dreams, fantasies...the wall opened and Joseph Glazman came in to talk to me. Borka Friedman came to me and he said, "I'll see you, I'll wait for you in Rudnik *Puszcza*, Jungle." This was where the partisans were organizing. My family told me that I said things in my sleep, but this I don't remember.

After I overcame the pneumonia, Fanya and I got married by a rabbi. When we were younger we were often in the same group of friends, though she was younger than me. We all knew each other. We spoke about maybe leaving the ghetto. Fanya's parents told me they didn't want her to go into the woods unwed.

I was promised a private room as our own apartment, but Abba Kovner from Shomer Ha'tzair beat me to it. He gave it to his brother. So when we got married, we even couldn't go for the honeymoon. She went to her mother and father, and I went home to my parents.

The FPO chose, first of all, young single people, young adults to leave the ghetto. Married couples also went. The only one that left his wife behind, that I remember, was Borka Friedman. I remember because we in the FPO had problems with her. When he left for the woods, she didn't return home because she knew that he went to the partisans. She was ill, physically ill; not serious, but sick enough for her not to go. She stayed with Benjamin Jacobson's sister to hide out in case the ghetto police looked for her. Sure enough, the police sought after her because they found out her husband, Borka Friedman, had disappeared.

The ghetto police, who didn't always agree with the FPO, said they would arrest her. The FPO hid her for about a week, and then the FPO tried to straighten the matter out with the Jewish authorities, and the ghetto chief of police.

Only three people knew where she was; Benjamin Jacobson, his sister, and me. The FPO told me one day, at 11 o'clock in the morning, I should bring her to a marked point. They said she was going to go to the ghetto jail for two hours, to have it on record that she was arrested. They promised that in two hours she would be released. She'd never stay there overnight. The Germans often came to the precinct jails at night and whoever was behind bars, they would take to Ponary.

When I brought her to the piazza that was arranged, she was arrested and taken to the precinct on Litzkah Street. When I first entered the piazza, I saw faces watching in the windows around this little courtyard. I even saw a gun. So I knew right away that the FPO was watching out for us. And that was what it was. I left her there. I had to walk out by the gate. I was not to say anything. The police came in and took her away to the jail on Litzkah Street where she was booked. In one hour, she was released. Otherwise there would have been a fight in the ghetto between the FPO and the Jewish police.

At this time, there was even more concern to take out as many Jews as possible. The FPO now took up to thirty people at a time, but never all from the same work group. From, like thirty people, maybe from as many as twenty or thirty different work units, so one or two from each group wouldn't be missed. We left early in the morning so it looked like I was taking them to work. We carried guns with us. We walked, there were certain places, work-places, out-of-town, like Beallahvakah. There was a torf where bricks were made from the mud. Past Beallahvakah was another group of workers cutting wood. There were maybe sixty or seventy workers there. Our friend, Mollie Kiejdan, worked there.

Nobody knew except for those people who were not returning to ghetto. So what I did seemed normal.

We didn't have to hide till we reached the workplaces. When we came to the last workplace, it was already getting dark. We slept there for the night. My workers were not allowed to talk to anybody, no one. It was known that we were going to open another place to cut lumber, so I was supposedly leading this group to the new place. If the question came up, where were the tools, I had an answer. We needed the saws, so I would have said they were being delivered by a horse and wagon. Thank G-d I was never stopped with a group of workers.

Whatever time I came back to the ghetto, it was okay. If I came in the morning it was okay, in the evening, okay. I could go away for a day and a half, or even two. I was my own boss. I was assigned to help out the *Arbeitsabteilung*, the Labor Department. So whatever I did, I always said it was for the Labor Department and no one in the ghetto police department, not even my superiors, questioned me. Some members of the police department were also FPO members; some were not.

Sometimes we paid the two Lithuanian policemen who stay by the ghetto for letting out such a big group. The FPO planned the operation, but we had no connection with the people in the woods. Once you arrived, you had to find your own connection, either with a partisan group or with a commander of a group, or form your own group.

Once, for example, I took the group into the woods, into the Rudnik Jungle. For us to get to the jungle took two nights of walking, marching. During the day, we had to hide so nobody would see us. If somebody saw us, we detained them for as long as possible. We couldn't let them go till dark, when we were safe to move. We didn't harm anyone though. Otherwise we would have had the people from the surrounding neighborhoods against us.

It happened once with a boy that had a herd of cows. The cows and the boy didn't come back on time, so the farmer went out to look for them. After dark we sent the farmer and his son one way, and we went the other.

Once I took Grishka Gurwicz's group past the village of Sorok Tatar. From there I showed them the way to go south, that was all to it. And I came back. I took them past Sorok Tatar till the house of Tatar Villikan, and he led them to the woods.

Then one or two months later, I took Grishka's mother to the jungle, with his aunt, a very beautiful girl. There were other families whom I took to the jungle. Grishka Gurwicz survived. His mother, though, was killed by the Polish army. She was in hiding, but was found by a Polish family, by a gentile family, so the White Polish army cut her up in pieces.

In July or August of the summer of '42, I took out Joseph Glazman's group. I led groups out at least ten different times, maybe twelve. Now every few weeks the FPO would arrange for a group to go. I led groups by the train to New Vilna at least three times; I led three groups to Tatar Villikan; and I walked out of the ghetto leading groups three or four times. We arranged sometimes with farmers, sometimes with garbage collectors, to hide our guns and meet us outside the ghetto. The guns were hidden in their wagons. One or two of us stayed with the guns and the rest I led out of the ghetto using my papers. I led Borka Friedman's group, Grishka Gurwicz's group, the sergeant's group, Fifke di Pomele was in a group, Kiejman Karer's group; I led, at least two hundred fifty to three hundred people out of ghetto and into the woods.

Joseph Glazman's group I led by train to New Vilna. After a day of work, instead of coming back by train, Glazman's group went north. Dessler found out that a group of Jews were heading north and reported it to the Gestapo. Joseph Glazman had asked everyone in his group to take no documents with them, but some people did. For safety sake, the documents were gathered and kept with one person in the group. Joseph Glazman was unaware of this. He never would have allowed it. Two days later, as they travelled north, they came to a bridge and the Germans were waiting for them. Six or more were killed. Everyone in Glazman's group ran into the woods in different directions. One of those killed was the one carrying the documents. Your mother's cousin, Israel Dupczanski, had given documents to this person.

The Germans came into the ghetto and rounded up every family member of from the documents they had found, and took them straight to Ponary, the shooting grounds where the Germans killed the Jews. Your mother lost many people in her family. Israel Dupczanski survived the war and worked in the Tzecka Party after the war. He was in a position where he was in charge of supplies.

After this incident, I made one hundred percent sure that no one in any group I led out of the ghetto had any identification papers with them, no photographs, no papers, no documents – nothing.

Some people hid in the sewers of Vilna to escape. Chana and Ruby Raichel, Etta and Simon Lichtenstein were some. Etta's father Israel was with them too. Chana and Ruby hid in the sewers for eleven months. There were more people, but I don't remember who.

In September of 1943, one month before the Germans surrounded the ghetto I was taken off the police force. The chief of police, the assistant ghetto chief, Dessler, accused me of meeting once in the past with Borka Friedman. We had been coming out from a FPO meeting. They knew that Borka Friedman was the head of the Beitar. They also knew Borka Friedman went to the partisans, and left his wife in the ghetto.

The night Dessler also accused me of meeting with Nathan Ring. It had been late, past curfew and after my police duties. Nathan Ring was a captain from the first precinct and I had no business with him, officially. Dessler fired whomever he had only an *achshod*, a suspicion, that he was from the FPO, so Dessler fired me. The disagreements between the ghetto police and the FPO were worse than ever.

Everyone was so surprised in the Labor Department, that they asked me, "Is it true? Are you a member of the FPO?" and I still denied it. The Labor Department didn't take away my documents so I continued to lead groups out into the woods.

In October of 1943, the ghetto was surrounded by the Germans. On the first of the three days, I had to take out all the guns and run to the meeting place, the *bod*, a bathing place. Anyway, I couldn't carry both boxes, so I took out one. There were about twenty-five guns in each. Lolkah, my older brother, was sitting in the yard. He asked what I was carrying.

I told him, "It's a box with guns and I have to take it to the *bod*, but I have another box downstairs."

He said, "Get it."

I got it out. I carried one box and he carried the other box, and this is how he got into the fighting group of the FPO, and joined the partisan group. Certainly, I had my own two guns, both Belgians with fourteen bullets. I kept one and gave the other to Lolkah. And from this moment on, Lolkah and I stuck together like glue.

The Germans surrounded the ghetto. Then they came in and took out the young adult men to concentration camps. The men were loaded up on trucks and brought to the railroad station. They were taken out to concentration camps in Estonia. That's what happened to Ruby Wagner and David Hamburg.

During the first day, when the Germans surrounded the Vilna ghetto,

Lolkah and I, and some others, were running around with the guns. The FPO ordered us not to shoot.

I was on *Strashun in Bod*. We didn't like it there because it was too open. These bathing places were very large.

Another group, on the other side of the ghetto, was also ordered not to shoot by the FPO. There were about maybe six or eight members of the FPO with guns there. They were ordered not to shoot, and the Gestapo came there and took them away. They followed FPO orders, but were taken to labor camps.

I was ordered to stay in *Strashun in Bod*, but I didn't. It didn't feel safe. With guns we went to look for our commanders. My commander was Yechiel Shaynberg. We didn't find him, but in the street we saw Ganz with one of the police lieutenants. And they saw us. We were a group of six, seven, or maybe even eight. It was Lolkah, Byonke Adelson, Moshe Niperholtz, and some others, along with me. Anyway, Ganz pulled out his gun and started shooting at us. But what we didn't know was that the Germans were also on this street. Maybe Ganz shot at us to show the Germans that he would shoot at Jews.

We shot back and started turning back towards our position in *Strashun in Bod*. On the way, we ran by a police station. They saw us running with the guns. Those policemen ran away when they saw us. I am talking about the Jewish police. It happened that Yechiel Shaynberg, our commander, was right next to them in the first building past the police station. We didn't know it though. He was killed later that same evening in a shootout with the Germans, with the Gestapo. They shot him through the throat, and then put a bomb in the building and blew it up. Then the Germans left the ghetto.

Ganz rounded up all the policemen that were in the precinct that we had run through. He put them on a truck and sent them out of the ghetto, because they allowed my brother and me—they called us the Varshavtchik group—to run through the streets. Ganz gave those policemen out to the Germans as punishment, because they let us run through the precinct. I think they either got sent to concentration camps, or were killed.

That's why we sent word to Ganz and to Dessler, and to all the officers in the police department. "If somebody touches my parents just because of me, I'm gonna come in and shoot everybody in the *khilah*, in the office, of the *Judenrat*, the Jewish government." No man could walk in the street at that time; but I don't remember, with either Sonya Madayska or with somebody else from the FPO, or even with the head of the FPO, we got word to Ganz and Dessler.

During the last two days of the liquidation, the FPO locked us in a *maline*, in a hiding place, because they didn't want us running around in the ghetto with guns in our hands. We didn't give away our guns, but they simply didn't want us in the street.

We were in hiding the three days. We were in an FPO gathering place, but not our usual place. The Jewish police wouldn't dare come over to us. They knew that we had guns, we were armed. The Jewish police helped the Germans round up men, but they knew they had to stay out of our neighborhood. The police had a big job to prevent fighting from breaking out in the ghetto. The FPO and the ghetto police each had their own ideas about how to save as many of us as possible. We didn't always agree.

How could we do what we did? I don't know if this is the answer: we just weren't afraid. We had nothing to fear because nobody believed we would survive. If you went up to anyone in those days and said you were going to survive, we would spit you in your face and say you were a liar. Nobody thought we would survive.

Chapter 6: The Partisans

After the Germans took enough men for the labor camps, after the three days, the blockade was over. The Germans left. Fanya, your mother, knew exactly where we were, and she was sitting outside, waiting for us to come out of the hiding place. When we came out, we had a meeting with the FPO. We had to leave the ghetto as soon as possible. Fanya said she must go home to say goodbye to her parents. I went with her. I said goodbye to her father. Her mother came over to me and said, *"Du zolst nor zayn gut tsu ir."* You should only be good to her. That's all she said. "Hirshala, I just want you to be good to her." That's all.

The day before we left the ghetto, we arranged with our housekeeper Vera that she should take in my parents and Yechial. Vera lived in a single house by the cemetery. My family could hide there. Lolkah and I left with a clear conscience that nothing was going to happen to our parents.

It was late on an October evening, in the year 1943. We had no extra clothes whatsoever because it was decided very quickly. In fact, I just went home and said goodbye to Father and Mother and told them we were leaving. They were outside the house. I didn't even come inside. Lolkah did the same thing. He must have run into the house to say goodbye to Jenke, to his wife and to his daughter. And we went out.

It was arranged by the FPO in conjunction with the ghetto police. The Nazis were liquidating the ghetto, killing off the elderly and the ill, so the groups became bigger and bigger. We had to get out as many as we could.

The Jewish police stood right there—right there at the gate. The Lithuanian police were on the other side of the ghetto gate. We walked out almost as one large group. There were about forty of us. We walked out as if we were workers going to a work site. Nobody questioned us.

We walked up the hill in Vilna to the first crossroad, two blocks from the ghetto gate. From there we went out by twos, a boy and a girl whenever it was possible. There should be a distance between each group. Benjomka Jacobson, a tall fellow, he walked with Fanya as a couple, I remember. I was in the front. I was the first one to go out. Two went on the left-hand side; two went on the right-hand side—on the sidewalk, not in the street—to hide that we were Jewish. Bieniek Lewin was in the group. The brothers Czuzoj, and their mother too. It was all arranged. Nobody had to stop. Not one of us had to stop.

We had a farmer who would take out our guns in a wagon, but we didn't trust him, so Lolkah and two others walked with the farmer and the wagon. The idea was that nobody should carry a gun in the street outside the ghetto. So all the guns were put in a bag in the wagon.

As soon as we walked away, a block from the ghetto gate, we took off the yellow star of David. We had a star like on a thin piece of paper. We tore it off and threw it away. We arranged to meet outside the city, near Porubanek, by the big white cross. It was like a *matka boska*, a landmark, a crossroads sign with Jesus on it. It was three kilometers from the ghetto. There we met up with Lolkah, the others and the farmer. We distributed the guns and the farmer headed back with an empty wagon.

Not everybody from the FPO could get out the first night. Each night went a group, as many as could go. Some got caught. Sonya Madayska was caught. She had a public hanging in the cemetery. Voydek, an engineer, was a member of the FPO. He was caught and they hung him too.

We came to Tatar Villikan's house. I brought everybody to his house and he came out and didn't let us stay even five minutes. He got dressed immediately and led the way to the jungle, into the forest. He took my group a short distance then left us to continue on our own.

I led the group all the way into the jungle. We walked at night. During the day we hid. Berta Bilbinder, she came as a nurse with her husband, Mottle. Bieniek Lewin was the youngest one from our group. He had a small caliber handgun, an automatic pistol. He was playing with his gun in his pocket and he gave out one shot. The bullet went into somebody's arm, but didn't touch the bone. Otherwise, the man would have lost his arm. I took away Bieniek's gun.

The next morning, we met people in the woods. We met *Bakishstah*, which means father, Biela Bierofka, the white bearded one, a leader of another partisan group. He had been a teacher, but was now a commander of a group of

Russian partisans. He said he could not stay with us, could not help us because, the thing was, we had walked into the woods right behind the Germans. It was a miracle. The Germans went in front; we had just walked behind them. Biela Bierofka said he would return soon, after the danger of the soldiers had passed.

The Polish people who lived just before the jungle, on the outskirts, knew that the Germans were there. They were happy to see us come in. They thought the Germans would kill us.

Biela Bierofka came to us the next day. We were on a hilltop in the swamps of the jungle. He brought four or five rifles. He said if he could he'd get more rifles, if we had money to buy from the gentiles. We didn't have money.

Biela Bierofka told us the Russian partisans couldn't move us because he didn't know yet exactly where the Germans were or what their plans were. Maybe the Germans were staying in a nearby village; maybe just passing through. He advised us not to move from this hilltop for at least another day. He said that when he learned something, he'd send word to us that we can move around. Biela Bierofka also told us we should wait until more of the organized partisans, the Russians, came back to the jungle. And certainly, as newcomers to the jungle, we didn't know anything. We did just as he said to do.

We didn't have to hide anymore in the daytime. In the jungle, we were free to move around, day or night. In fact, we sneaked to the edge of the jungle in the day, and stayed at the edge until it got dark and then moved further into the jungle. Each of us had one set of clothing. Fanya had a rubber raincoat, which was a lifesaver for us.

Two days later, another group came. We were in a village, about five kilometers from our base, looking for food, about five of us—Lolkah and me, and I don't remember who else. It was dark. We heard voices. Lolkah jumped out in the middle of the road and said, "*Stoy, idyot.*" Stop, who's coming? More partisans were arriving from the ghetto. We brought them to the same base, to the hilltop in the swamp.

The Russian partisans started returning. They had left the jungle because the Germans had come in just before us. The Russian partisans told us to break up our camp, to make groups, and make different bases, like one hilltop here and one hilltop there. They told us to move two kilometers further where it was a little higher and dryer. We settled in the Rudnitska Woods, approximately one hundred twenty kilometers west by southwest of Vilna. The Russians had a lot more experience. They knew these woods, so we listened to their advice. They were ex-Russian soldiers. The Russian army was no longer in this part of the country. Many of these soldiers had been prisoners of war captured by the Germans, and they had escaped. They wanted to fight the Germans.

Each day after that, for the next three days another group came from Vilna, about thirty people each time. The last group that came was the largest, eighty people came. Abba Kovner came in one of the last groups to arrive. Along with the leaders of the Tzecka Party, the communist party, Abba Kovner formed a headquarters. They were the leaders of the FPO in Vilna. We were divided in to four *ahtrods*, fighting groups. Each group had a different name. One was "To Be Free," another "Fight Fascism," another "For Victors." My group's name, we were in the second ahtrod, I don't remember. The leaders were in the first ahtrod and took the biggest island in the swampy jungle to make a headquarters. I was two kilometers away atop another hill. It was just a little dry circle of land. If you put in a shovel two inches, you reached water already. The third and fourth ahtrod were sent a little further away from the headquarters, to a dry section of the jungle.

Biela Bierofka, the first commander we met, helped us in many ways. He taught us how to get food. He helped us organize the partisan movement. Biela Bierofka was the first one to take us to a railroad track and teach us how to blow it up. Two or three of his men taught us how to use grenades, how to use dynamite, and how to use the fuses. The dynamite, for example, was not detonated by water, cold or heat. You could burn it and it wouldn't blow up. The fuse, on the other hand, could be destroyed by water, detonated by the heat, and even detonated by any drastic movement. There was, by us, a boy from Kovna, Chaim Lazar, he was holding the fuse. He played with it, and the fuse blew up his hand.

When we blew up our first train we were so stupid. Immediately we ran to the train to look for weapons, a rifle, a pistol, even a pair of boots. It was so dangerous; we could have been killed, but we learned.

We didn't go by our right names in the woods. Everyone knew me as Gregory Barisovitz. In the woods, people who already knew you used your right name. We had no papers. Nobody had any papers at all. We kept no papers and changed our names to protect the families we left behind in Vilna.

Whoever knew me called me Hirshka. The Russians, when they came, called me Grisha. The farmers called me Gregory Barisovitz.

At first we just slept on the ground, even in the snow. Fanya's rubber raincoat was our bed, our mattress, our protector from the dampness. It wasn't until the end of the winter in 1943 that we built bunkers to sleep in. There weren't many women in our group, but those that were there were fighters. We were a mixed group. There were about forty of us, Jews, Russians, Lithuanians, and even one person from Holland in our ahtrod. He joined us when we blew up a train. He had been a prisoner of war. He ran from the train and joined us.

When we were in the woods, different groups of Russian partisans came to us to pick out people that they needed for their groups. So we stood up on the hill, a line of twenty, for example; and they came over and said, "Okay, you come with me, you come with me, and you come with me. That's it. That's all we need."

Everybody was happy to go, to be useful, in the partisan movement. Lolkah was picked to be in a group that used explosives. They had dynamite sent to them from Moscow. The only thing they did was blow things up: blow up trains, blow up bridges. That was all they did. Constantly. Lolkah's base was just past the first ahtrod, the headquarters. From the first ahtrod to Lolkah's base you walked across felled logs placed in the swamps to get to his island, just one hundred meters away, very close.

Dynamite was dropped in. The Russian partisans who had taken Lolkah with them, buried it in different places. Only they knew where it was. They took out whatever they needed, but they never gave us even one chance to blow up a train. Unlike Biela Bierofka, they didn't trust us. We had no training. Their commander was a Russian captain. He had different units in different places; their only job was to blow up trains and bridges. I saw Lolkah very seldom, only by chance.

In the woods I was a *razwietctzik*, a scout. I went to the villages. I had my connections with the farmers to find out if there was a new movement from Germans any place. I knew this connection who traveled regularly to Vilna. I asked, "What did you see, a military movement, soldiers on the road?"

The farmers told me, not because they liked me, but because they were afraid of me. They knew I was from Vilna or Kovna. They knew right away I was Jewish. I always had a gun with me. No one ever turned me in, thank G-d.

The farmers also knew I was fair, that I was honest and fair. For example, if I came to a village and I said, "I need from you two hundred pounds of flour, and two hundred pounds of potatoes," I gave them a receipt. So, at the end of the war, if there was to be a payment for this food, the farmer could go to the government and say, "I have a receipt that this food was taken from me." After the war they could claim that they helped the partisans. I signed the receipt in the name of Gregory Barisovitz. I put out a lot of good connections while I was a scout.

I even sent food to Vera, our former housekeeper, and her family in Vilna. If a Polish farmer was going to Vilna, I went to him, saying, "Look, this is for Vera." And I asked Vera should get us medicine. The farmer used to sleep in our house, above the bakery. Our house was left open.

Vera had an apartment somewhere by herself with her husband and child. From Vilna, she sent me the medicine - aspirin, iodine, and sometimes bandages. The iodine was what we needed most, to keep wounds from becoming infected. But if somebody got shot in the stomach and the bullet didn't go through, the bullet was still there. There was nothing we could do. We had no hospital. We had no medicine for this.

Eventually, we were able to get our own dynamite from Moscow. The dynamite was parachuted to the Lithuanian brigade of the Russian partisans. The Lithuanian partisan commanders came and gave us the dynamite. Most of them were actually Jewish, but at the time we didn't know.

I blew up trains. I blew up train track, anything to stop the Germans. There was a group of us, three men and two women; one was Mania Kaplan. The women were as good as the men. One time we set out to blow up railroad track one quarter kilometer from a bridge. The Germans didn't trust the Lithuanian army, so the Germans themselves were guarding the bridge. We knew we could destroy the track leading to the bridge. We were thirty kilometers east of Jurbarkas on the Neman River.

Before we came to the railroad track, we stopped at a nearby partisan base. We told them where we were going to do. Their leader told us that an extra reinforcement of Germans had just arrived at the railroad station near the bridge. This partisan group decided to leave their base because what we were doing was putting them in danger. They felt that what we were doing was wrong, but we were not the ones to decide to do it, or not to do it. We were sent to do it, and that's all there was to it. We were sent. We did it.

The two women in our group were holding a farmer we came upon who knew the neighborhood. They tied him up with a rope and held onto the rope so he shouldn't run away from them. We put up a hundred pieces of dynamite by a crossing where two railroad tracks met. We put up a piece of dynamite and the *palnic*, the fuse. The wick we cut from parachutes. Once you lit it, you couldn't put it out. Once all the dynamite was set, we had to light all the wicks. But, it was a lot to light you know, on both sides of the track. You ran from one to the other, to the other, to the other. The wick was about two inches long. It took about five minutes to burn. There was a hole in the fuse that you stuck the wick into. The fuse was very sensitive, so when the heat of the wick burned close to the fuse, it blew up the fuse, and the fuse blew up the dynamite.

As soon as you lit the last one, you started running. But you had to know which direction to run to safety. The farmer was still being held by Mania Kaplan and the other woman. And every time a piece of dynamite exploded, we counted to see how many explosions there were. After the track was destroyed we let the farmer go and returned to the woods.

During the winter of 1943-44, the headquarters of the Vilna partisans decided that this area could not sustain so many partisans, so they split us in half. Half would stay in the same place in Puszcza Rudnicka, the Rudnitska Woods, and half would be sent further west on the way to East Prusy toward Austbrausin, closer to the Germans, to try to organize there a partisan movement. The leaders picked one hundred twenty; Fanya and I were among them. There also was Zelda Botwinik in this group. Berta and Mottle Bilbinder, that I mentioned, were in this group too.

We were one hundred twenty when we left. Chaim Lazar led us. He's the one who lost his right hand when a fuse blew up in it. That was Chaim Lazar. Smulkah Berenstein was there. We had three machine guns, the light type of machine gun. We had maybe ten or twelve rifles. We had maybe ten or twelve guns. It was to be a long walk, maybe one hundred to one hundred thirty kilometers.

As we walked we came to Natcha, which was very, very dangerous, because based there were twelve or thirteen thousand White Polish soldiers each with a *horshel*, an eagle, on their helmet. They had machine guns, heavy machine guns. They had rifles. For example, for each rifle we had, we had only ten bullets. They had two hundred bullets. So it was not to compare our strength of the one hundred twenty hungry to their strength.

The White Polish soldiers never fought the Germans. In fact, they used to get their guns and ammunition from the Germans. Supposedly the British were supplying the Polish with weapons to fight the Germans. From what we could see, the White Polish army was supplied by the Germans so they could fight the Jews.

Natcha was the most horrible place that you could ever think. For thirty days, we didn't even taste a little warm water. For thirty days, we didn't take off our boots. We were always on the move. This was in January of 1944.

We just couldn't stay in one place more than two or three hours because of the Polish army. We came to one place, and in two hours, the Polish army was right behind us. It was winter, and we heard them coming. We turned and went into the swamps. Fortunately, there was an *ahtoemon*, a mist, a fog over the swamps. The soldiers couldn't see us. We stood there maybe for five hours up to our necks in the water. The water itself didn't feel cold, but the ground, the bottom of the water had ice. Many of us lost our boots in the mud. Our feet were so numb we just kept walking. So no wonder some had to get their toes, some their feet, amputated later, when we finally returned in February to our base in the Rudnik Puszcza.

During the month of January, in Natcha, I decided to try to find some food. There was a young teenager from Swienciany, Grishiyuka Misheyitska. He was maybe fifteen, sixteen years old. I said to him, "Do you want to come with me? We'll go. We'll try to bring some food, some bread?" because people were really hungry.

He said, "Sure."

So, we went to the commanding officers and said they shouldn't leave this place, because we wanted to go and try to bring back food. We went out. We came to a village, a big village with houses on both sides of the street. It was either a Friday or a Saturday, when they baked bread. A loaf of bread was a *pud*, twelve kilos. You could smell in the air the fresh-*kite*, freshness of the baked bread.

At the very first house, hanging by the door was a Polish soldier's hat, without the big eagle. There was a small eagle. No one was home so I stole this hat and wore it. We went on to another house. The people inside saw we were with rifles, machine guns, whatever, and we told them we needed a horse and wagon. If it was in the barn they were not going to deny it. Right away they hitched the horse to the wagon. They knew that when I let the horse go he would return to their barn with the wagon.

We tromped into house after house and spoke Polish saying, "*Bug Zaplac.*" That means G-d will pay you back in good measure. We came for food, we came for bread. And in every house we were given a loaf, or half a loaf of a twelve-kilo bread.

We spoke in Polish. They didn't know we were partisans. They assumed we were part of the Polish army. I had the hat that I took out from the first house, and I went in and said, "*Bug Zaplac.*" We came back with one hundred twenty loaves of bread.

We unloaded the wagon by the woods. We let the horse go back, because in swamps we didn't need a horse and wagon. It was, how should I tell you, it was a *Simchas Torah*, the joyous dancing because G-d gave the Jewish people the Torah. The way everybody was right away eating the bread, it was like a new life came into them.

The next night, the leaders decided somebody should go back to Rudnik Puszcza to find out if we could come back, because here, we could not get organized. We couldn't fight the White Polish army. There were too many of them. The guns that we had compared to their guns, it was crazy to think we could fight.

I volunteered to go. It had been my turn to go on post, on guard duty. So the leader canceled my guard duty. I prepared for the trip back to Rudnik Puszcza. I said goodbye to Fanya and arranged to have someone who should walk with her and watch her.

We heard a shot, one shot. Right away we all got up together. Somebody ran from the post, from my post. He said, "Majshe Icke got killed!" Majshe Icke was the one who had taken my place.

He said, "Majshe Icke got killed! The Polish are coming!" So right away we began running away from there. As we ran we heard more shots, like warning shots, or whatever. We came to a fork in the road. Left or right? To the left, it seemed that the road led to the bushes, to a dead end. To the right was a well-traveled path. This was the way to go.

There was one boy that knew the place very well. He said, "No, we cannot go to the right. They are pushing us to go that way. There is a farm on top of the hill. That's where they are hiding with machine guns. They will kill us all off like nothing!" He had a feeling. He had a feeling. We knew the house on top of the hill, but the boy insisted saying, "This is a trick. They are trying to chase us there, to the top of the hill where they have machine guns."

So we went, we went, to the left, past the bushes, down a two-track wagon trail. Snow began falling. There was the sound of a wagon coming toward us, on a farmer's road. I was always the first one up front. I lifted my hand. Everybody dove and hid between the little trees that were on the right side.

The farmer came through sitting sideways on the wagon, not facing the horse, sitting with his back to us. He didn't see us. The wagon from both sides had wooden slats, very much like ladders. You put one down and sat sideways, turning your head to see the road. In this manner he passed us by without seeing us.

In about two minutes, we heard the wagon stop behind us. We heard noises and it started snowing even heavier. The Polish soldiers stopped the wagon and asked this farmer if he had seen a group of Jews. Those in the rear of our group heard the conversation. The farmer said he saw nothing so the Polish soldiers set off in another direction.

Soon we were running out of the bushes following after the wagon tracks, continuing in the direction from which the farmer had come. The snow covered our footprints.

Further down the road, toward nightfall, in the woods we found a single farmhouse. That night we stayed on the farm. It was a big farm. There was a husband, a wife, and children. Certainly we were watching them, guards were set up, but we had no place else to go. We filled up the house and barn. And this is how we survived the night.

The four leaders from our group decided not to send me back to Rudnik. They said I should take eighty from the one hundred twenty, and go to Rudnik. The last night in Natcha, they came in and said to me they were staying and we should go. They would lead us out part of the way and then turn back. Forty should stay. They would try to find the one that was missing, Majshe Icke, who'd taken my place. They said maybe he was alive and they were going to look for him.

Those forty, they kept the best for themselves. They kept the four machine guns. The forty with shelter had all the machine guns and eight rifles. The eighty of us had no machine guns and only four rifles, and a winter's march.

It was February of 1944 when I brought my group back to the Rudnik Jungle. We walked for two days in the winter cold. I was busy with crossing the river with about seventy people, on foot. Fanya was left with a group of about ten, maybe even less, who walked much more slowly. I was busy with the larger group of people, leading them through the woods.

I knew this part of the jungle like my five fingers. I knew there was a crossroad that I have to pass over, and then continue straight. It was the middle of the night and it started to snow. We walked up and down the road. I could not find the crossing. I thought if it wasn't the crossing, I was in the wrong place. We walked another mile, maybe less than a mile, and still couldn't find the crossing.

So I thought we were lost. I said to everybody, "Lie down and sleep. We have to wait till morning." We lie down in the snow and fell asleep, all of us. When it got light, I saw we were maybe ten feet away from the crossing, ten feet away.

Before we came to our base we stopped in the *shtab*, the headquarters. When the commanders saw us, they were very disappointed that we couldn't stay there and organize a partisan movement. They were especially disappointed when they saw the officers had left us by ourselves. We came without guns, without machine guns.

So that was how we came to our base. The only thing we had was a half a loaf of bread, each one of us. About six or eight people had their toes amputated. Only a few of us were still able to walk. We were sick, very sick, and very weak.

Three of us went out for food that day. I even didn't think about where Fanya was. We came to a village. We picked up two wagons with food, and on the way to our base we stopped again at the headquarters. That was when I learned that Fanya was paralyzed from the waist down to her toes.

She had gotten paralyzed the last night before we returned to Rudnik. The freezing cold was just too much for her.

I asked a doctor here, many years later, how this could happen. He thought she may have become paralyzed because of fear. After a time, the fear could paralyze you.

Maishe Itke carried her over a burned down bridge, to a farmer. The bridge was broken. It was just a beam lying in the water.

Maishe had been a foreman in transport work. Before the war he had a wagon and a horse. If we needed flour, for example, we called him. He went to the mill and brought us the bags of flour. He was a big, very strong guy, like an elephant, so he carried Fanya across the river. Directly on the other side of the bridge was a little farm. The farmer tied up a horse to a wagon to carry the ones who couldn't walk, and gave Maishe Itke the reins. Itske Kulkin was in the wagon with Fanya.

The farmer said, "Go." The horse walked a short distance, turned around and came back. The farmer took them to the edge of the farm and again said, "Go." Three times the horse came back to the farmer. So the farmer led them maybe two miles down the road. The farmer said to them, "You cannot get lost. The partisans will find you. Once you're in the woods, the partisans will find you."

The leaders of our group, Abba Kovner, Yenke Borovka; none of them were happy to see us. They were all disappointed that we couldn't establish a new base nearer the Germans.

Lolkah, who lived nearby, had to pass through the headquarters in order to go to his base. Here, at the headquarters, they had already built a bunker, a roof over your head. You could lie down and sleep on dry ground. The commanders lived in the bunker. The rest of us lived out in the open. They put a barrel in the bunker for a fireplace. It was warm enough near the barrel, but the heat didn't fill up the whole space. The commanders decided to put Fanya right by the barrel. She was the closest one to the barrel. She was paralyzed for two to three months. In the end she was well-fed and well-cared for.

I didn't find out from Lolkah or Fanya what had happened. One of the partisans who had witnessed it told me. Fanya wasn't always by the barrel. At first, Fanya had been left outside the bunker. There was talk that since she was paralyzed anyway, and there wasn't much food, maybe it would be better for everyone if she didn't survive. There was talk of a doctor giving her an injection that would end her life. Word of this reached Lolkah who came through almost every day.

He entered the headquarters, laid down his machine gun on the commander's table and said, "I'll kill you all, you sons of a…if one hair falls from Fanya's head, I will kill you all!" Lolkah's eyes were like fire. They knew he meant every word. Lolkah they knew to be crazy. When there was a fight brewing, he ran to be in the battle. He never thought of his own safety. He stood out in the open firing his gun. He could out-drink the Russians he fought alongside. The commanders knew Lolkah would be true to his words. That was when Fanya was moved to be near the barrel.

Those forty who stayed behind at the farm for two months formed a base, like a partisan base. This farmer took them to rich farmers at night. They robbed those farmers and brought the food back: meat, whatever they needed; a cow, a pig—you know. Then they came back to his house. This farmhouse was in a place without neighbors, secluded, a good base.

When those forty came back to the Rudnik Jungle, we thought they would be shot or hung. But they weren't. We don't know exactly how or even if their leaders were disciplined because three of them were members of the Communist Party from before the war and had political connections.

When I came back to base I also found out that the day we left, Nathan Ring had been shot. He was a good leader, a good man. We heard stories about his death so since I knew Abba Kovner from Vilna I asked him what happened. He said he had voted against this action. However, as well as our commanders, we had a Russian political commander, Diddiallise who was trained by authorities in Russia. The political commander watched over five bases like ours. He was the eyes of the Tzecka Party.

Diddiallise was concerned that Nathan Ring would threaten the leadership. He and a group of five others took Nathan on a "mission." Nathan was told not to bring his handgun, a big Belgium with fourteen bullets, like mine. He was told they would stop by a base to pick up a machine gun for Nathan and two other people. Then they'd go on to blow up a train. Nathan Ring carried the dynamite.

The group walked two hundred feet from the base. A grave was already dug. The five opened fire. While wounded, Nathan Ring reached into his sock for a small gun. Before he could fire, one of the five shot him in the head. I knew Nathan Ring from the ghetto. He was a good man.

After returning to the base with the group of eighty, the leaders of the shtab gave us a new commander for our group. His name was Abrashka Reshl. He was called Sobrin in America, but in the woods his name was Reshl. He liked me very much and I liked him. I felt that, with him, it was safe to go, because he wasn't afraid. He wouldn't say, "You go." He would say, "We go," or "I go, and you watch me."

I liked very much to go with him whenever he asked me. One day, I had just come from being away from the base for three days scouting and looking for food. He called me over and said, "Hirshka, listen, I know you just came back. Go lie down and take a rest and sleep. You'll go with me tonight. We're going past Salki on the other side of the railroad tracks. We also have to send somebody to Popiszki, the nearby village."

I said to him, "If that's the way you want, that's the way it will be."

He didn't want to send me at all. There were two scouting actions to do. One scouting action, Popiszki, was about eight to ten kilometers from the base. While to go past Salki would take a day's walk, he said to me, "I know you're entitled to go to Popiszki, but I would like you to go with me."

That night we drove past Salki, into a rich Lithuanian village, to gather food. We had no other way to feed ourselves except to go to villages and take food. That night we left loaded up with maybe eight wagons of food: bread, flour, meat, butter and eggs, even with linen. We needed only to bring the wagons back to the base. I felt right away that this place was not safe because I didn't enter the houses; I stayed outside with the wagons while others gathered up the food. Since I remained outside, I better understood the movements at the edge of the village. I was begging them, "Come out, come away, let's go."

"Another minute, another minute, another minute." So we waited.

The whole time, three hours or whatever it took, I was all the time outside. I saw movement on the other side of the railroad track, so when they came out I said, "Don't let's cross here. Let's go a little further and cross over there." I told Abrasha, "I don't like the movement on the other side of the railroad track."

We had to cross the railroad track. There were fifteen of us with the eight wagons. I said, "Let's go to the next crossing. We shouldn't try to cross here. It's too much movement over there on the other side of the railroad track. It will take maybe five kilometers longer, but we'll go to the next crossing."

"No. What are you talking about?" everyone said. "What are you afraid of? What's the matter with you?"

I said, "I don't like the movement over there," but I couldn't get them to listen.

Sure enough, as soon as we got to the railroad track, as soon as we got to the crossing, the Lithuanian army or police started shooting. Abrasha and I, and a third guy, Shike Nemzer, we were up front. As a scout I am always in front.

I dove down as soon as I heard somebody pull back a clip. I knew already they were near and there would be shooting. It was winter and there was snow. I dove down and opened fire but, you know, at night it was hard to see. The soldiers were hidden there behind stacks of pallets where you couldn't see anybody. You couldn't aim at anything.

The partisans behind us left the wagons with the food, and ran away. They knew that five kilometers further down the road there was a crossing for us that was a safer place. Later, they told me that they tried to take two wagons, but the farmers were there and the farmers wouldn't let them.

But anyway, they ran away and we were left, the three of us, right by the railroad track. We crawled backwards down into the ditch beside the track. It was dangerous to go into the ditch, because it was mined, and you never knew where the mines were. So I said to the other two, "You run into woods. I'll use my machine gun to cover you. While I'm shooting, they're not going to shoot at you. When you're there, you shoot so I can come."

The two of them ran to the edge of the woods, but it was winter. It was snowing. The shooters could see us very easily, but as long as I was shooting, nobody would pick up their heads and look. Then when the other two reached the woods, they started shooting, and I joined them.

Afterwards, we snuck alongside the track. Then we heard a commotion between the soldiers and the farmers with the wagons. The farmers wanted to take the wagons back with the food, but the soldiers said, "No, that's ours because we saved it." The soldiers did not chase after us. They argued with the farmers.

We were running behind the trees, between the trees, right alongside the railroad track. Then, we heard a train coming. We stopped and it was a one-car train, a Panzer train. The train had the doors open. You could see inside maybe a dozen soldiers. They had machine guns. They even had a grenade launcher. So we let the train pass by and then we went across. As we crossed, I was the first and I told them, "You have to follow in my steps." Mines lined the railroad track. It was snow. Wherever I put the foot, that's where they put the foot, and we crossed the railroad track all right. We walked the five kilometers to the safe crossing, but we arrived home with nothing.

On the way home, I said to them, "Here is my brother's base. I want to stop in here. Maybe we'll sleep over till early morning, and then we'll go home." They said okay.

We came to the base and the guard said to me, "You cannot come in. There is trouble."

"What's the trouble?" I asked.

He said, "One guy got killed and one is wounded."

I asked, "Who got killed?"

He told me that the *starshina's*, the sergeant's, brother was killed. Lolkah was at that same base, but I didn't ask who was the wounded one. I didn't think to ask.

So they didn't let us in. We had to walk maybe another twelve kilometers. We walked, without a stop. Usually we stopped in Wiszyncy, the last village, about ten kilometers from our base. We usually stopped there at the house of the White Russian. He was sympathetic to us, but this time we kept going.

Usually we stopped for breakfast or for lunch, because the times I came from the road, I always dropped off food over there to store, so whenever I came I should have it. I went there when I was hungry and couldn't go to the base. I ate there, but I didn't eat their food, I ate my own food. When I came from the road, from a *zagatofke*, scouting for food with a wagon, I had to go through this village, so I picked something up from the wagon and always dropped it off there in the house, something: either a loaf of bread, a piece of cheese, a big chunk of meat, a lamb, something to save for another time. But this time we didn't stop.

A sled passed by carrying two people. One of them was Lonka Ryzow. I said, "This redhead is Lolkah's commander." He waved to me and I waved to him. He turned to speak to his captain, but only waved to me. They kept on going and we walked on to the base. I said, "We'll waste no more time. We have to reach the base as fast as we can." Somehow, I had a feeling to go home as quickly as I could.

When we came to the base Lonka Ryzow was waiting for me. He told me that Lolkah was wounded. He couldn't tell me earlier because he did not have his captain's permission. I told him, "We were just there, but the guard didn't let us in."

"Did he tell you that Lolkah is wounded?" he asked.

"No," I said. "I didn't ask who the wounded one was; I asked who was the dead one."

Lonka Ryzow said, "Lolkah is asking for his brothers."

Yechial was at another base, by the *shtab*, the headquarters. Yechial had escaped on the way to Ponary and had made his way to the partisans. My commander, Abrasha Reshl, the one who was with me on the last mission, said, "I want to go, too."

So we took the sleds and drove to Yechial. Yechial was at the base. He came with us back to the base where Lolkah was, but Lolkah was already dead. We never spoke to him. We didn't even have the chance to talk to him.

Lolkah was part of sixteen missions that blew up Nazi trains. He was mortally wounded on this his final mission.

The next morning, we dug out graves and we buried the two of them. Abrasha led us in saying *Kaddish*, the mourner's prayer, because it was so hard for us. We repeated it after him.

יִתְגַּדַּל וְיִתְקַדַּשׁ שְׁמֵהּ רַבָּא

"Yit-ga-dal ve-yit-ka-dash she-mei ra-ba...." Let G-d's name be made great and holy.... Yechial and I, we said Kaddish for Lolkah, for our eldest brother Lolkah.

That same night we found out that while we were going past Salki, Polish people from the village of Kaniuchi killed those two boys that went in my place to go to Popiszki. Those boys were sent just to check on what was going on in the neighborhood. The people from the village of Kaniuchi—Kaniuchi means one who raises horses—hated Jews.

So G-d was watching over me all those years, starting in Natcha when I volunteered to go back to the base and they sent somebody else in my place, to stand guard. G-d was watching over me all the way from the day the war broke out up until now. Thank you G-d.

It was in the beginning of 1944 when Yorgis came in. His real name was Ziman. In Lithuanian it was Zimanius. He was a Jew from Kovna. His name in the partisans was Yorgis. He had parachuted in from Moscow to a jungle east of Narocz. The Russian partisans and the Lithuanian partisans controlled different areas of the woods. Yorgis parachuted in with a group of Lithuanian partisans. Yorgis was the commander of the Lithuanian brigade.

Yorgis had connections with Moscow. He was the secretary of C.K. Party, the Lithuanian Communist Party. He was in charge of several bases. After he arrived, we had a mission, a big mission taped together for all of us; the Russians, the Lithuanians, and all the partisans that were available. It was known that one Polish village, Kaniuchi, got organized with the Germans. It was a big village, over one hundred houses there. The villagers got weapons from the Germans, and they were out to kill the Jews and the partisans.

The people of Kaniuchi used to come right to the edge of the jungle to try and catch partisans and kill them. They killed those two Jewish boys, and then they got so wild that they went as a mob to the village closest to the jungle, to Vichinsi, and did terrible things to the people in their houses. And then they left. Vichinsi was the first village outside the jungle, so certainly the villagers had to do whatever the partisans told them to do. The people of Kaniuchi terrorized those villagers.

The commanders of the shtab sent us out. At the time we left our base, nobody knew where we were going. Nobody knew what the mission was. All we knew was to meet near Kaniuchi. It was there that we would be given further instructions.

When we arrived, the leaders of the operation put us in groups and gave us numbers. They didn't say what every group had to do, they only gave us numbers; group one, group two, group three, group four, group five. We were told to hide in the woods until dark.

There were about one hundred twenty of us altogether. We met again, in the dark, at the outskirts of a village. We put up guards that no outsiders should come to listen to us, to the speeches of the commanders, who said, "We're going to a village." They didn't mention the name of the village.

"The village is two kilometers long. On its left side is a river. At the edge of the river they have a *banya*, a place where to take a bath. There was a bathhouse, a little house with stones inside. The stones were heated so the water could be warm.

"First of all, there is a group that has to break down the telephone *tsvias*, the telephone lines. Another group has to swing around the village and go in front, all the way in front, and make sure that nobody comes in or goes out. Then there is a group that watches the shore. If anyone swims to the other side of the river, they make sure nobody makes it alive to the other side."

I was in this group, by the river. "We take no prisoners. We take no food. We don't go in anybody's house to loot or ransack. Anything moves, we kill."

The partisans had talked to Moscow, and Moscow gave them the okay: we should go eliminate Kaniuchi. Not to take anybody alive, not to leave anything alive, and not to bring back anything from the village.

Until we were divided into groups we didn't know it was Kaniuchi. When we finally heard, "This is Kaniuchi," it was, what should I tell you? When you mentioned the name of Kaniuchi in the woods, it made us shake. We were so afraid of their vicious rage.

And then there were two groups, groups number four and five, who carried the torches, to burn. They burned - we burned the village to the ground so that not one house, not one shed, not one barnyard was left standing. As far as we knew, nobody was left alive.

I was never afraid that I would die. I thought if my time came that at least I would take someone with me. I was never afraid to do dangerous things. I did what I needed to do.

A few months after Yorgis came, soon after we burned Kaniuchi to the ground, the White Polish army surrounded our part of the Rudnik Jungle. The White Polish army gave out an order that everybody can go east to Minsk, to Russia, unharmed – every partisan except the Jews.

Yorgis radioed the Lithuanian government in Moscow. He gave them an ultimatum, "If you don't send us help, we have to leave the jungle. We are the furthest ones west, the closest to the Germans." When Yorgis spoke of us – he meant all the partisans, the Russians, Lithuanians, and the Jews. The Russians finally agreed and parachuted guns to us. They delivered food, *Svinayeka shomka* canned meat like Spam, medicine, tobacco and even two doctors. The Russians dropped machine guns and bullets. Supplies were parachuted from the skies. It was like manna from heaven.

The Lithuanian brigade sent us so many weapons we didn't know what to do with them. We had to bury them in the ground. We had more machine guns than we had people to use them, not guns, machine guns. *Avtomats*...I carried with me a bag of five hundred bullets. I had bullets that you could use and nobody would hear shots. I had bullets that if they hit a tree, they would tear it apart. I even had bullets that two of them could start a house on fire.

When I came to the jungle, I had three bullets in my rifle—three. When we went to Natcha, I had three bullets in my rifle. Now I walked with a bag of five hundred bullets. We had so much ammunition that we had to bury it.

Remember, we were surrounded. We were at that time one thousand, maybe twelve hundred partisans in the whole jungle. We were surrounded by the White Polish army: sixteen thousand soldiers. The White Polish army was famous for killing Jews. They were famous for killing Jewish children, Jewish women; cut them up in pieces. If they found a farmer that hid a Jew the soldiers would burn the farmhouse to the ground. To the partisans in Rudnik the White Polish army was ten thousand times worse than the Germans.

For three nights in a row, three nights in a row, the Russian planes came, and that was it. Everybody could see it and hear it from afar, especially when the airplanes cruised and made one drop, then cruised and made the other drop. Most of the White Polish army disappeared. Now that we had weapons the White Polish army just disappeared.

It was on the first of these three nights of parachuting supplies that a radio operator parachuted to us. I didn't know his name. I didn't know anything about him. I brought him to the shtab to Yorgis and that was it.

Years later, in the late 1960s, Borka Botwinik invited us to a party. He told us he had invited a lot of friends from the Lithuanian brigade. As we walked into Borka's house, this little guy was telling a story. He was talking about Yorgis. I said to him, "How do you know Yorgis?"

"Eh, what do you mean, how do I know Yorgis?" And he told me he was a radio operator and he was dropped into the jungle. But he was with Yorgis only two nights.

I said to him, "Were you caught in the tree? Was your parachute caught?"
"Yeah."
"Did somebody cut you down?"
He said, "Halfway, halfway." He fell down the other halfway by himself.
"Do you remember me?"
"No."

"Do you know that I'm the one that cut you down?"

"Oh, my G-d," he started to cry. I found out his name was Lofka.

When I first found him he thought I was a German. He was stuck in a tree and he heard some of us speaking Yiddish which he mistook for German. He thought he was parachuting into an area controlled by the Russian army so he was expecting to hear Russian. Now that he heard what he thought was German, he had his gun out ready to shoot himself so he wouldn't be captured. I didn't have to convince him of anything. Once I talked in Russian he put his gun away.

Lofka told me a story about going to the airport to board the airplane before being parachuted into the Rudnik Jungle. His driver, the one taking him to the plane, said to him, "Give me your belt. For that belt I can get two pair of shoes for my children."

"How can I give you the belt?" Lofka asked. "I need the belt."

The driver answered, "If you're going to live there two days, it'll be a lot."

After two nights with Yorgis, the Lithuanian partisans took him much further west. There he had connections with German families that would hide him. He had to radio information to Russia about the movement of the trains. But he also knew he could not stay in one place for more than one night. The Germans were listening to his radio signals and trying to track him down.

Who would think, after so many years, that we would meet? We are still friends.

I was in Popiszki speaking with a farmer when I heard a commotion outside. Popiszki was the first village you came to when you left jungle going east or south. I often brought back food from there. There was shooting outside. Another partisan group had been ambushed by White Polish soldiers. There was a partisan lying on the ground. He had been shot in the leg. I ran to him and *schlepped* him, half-carried, half-dragged him, to the nearest house. It was Yorgis. I lifted him onto a wagon and drove the horse into the woods to bring Yorgis back to our base. He was shot in the right leg, below the knee, in the calf muscle. There was no broken bone. Yorgis would be fine.

In the spring of '44, our commanders sent five of us back to Natcha, the same place we tried to establish a new base the previous winter. We didn't know ourselves why we were going, why they would send us back to Natcha. It was like sending us on a suicide mission. We found out afterwards that there was supposed to be a family living among gentiles and the family was paying the gentiles a lot of gold to keep them hidden. So instead of paying gold to the Polish family that was hiding them, the commanders wanted to bring the family here so the partisans should have the gold. But we never found the family. Of the five of us only one knew why we were going, only one. If we only knew, we would never have gone.

We made it there, believe it or not, in one day. We left the base early in the morning and went to Salki. We arrived in the village just about dawn. We walked all night from there to Natcha. All night. We didn't stop for a minute. We crossed three rivers. The water was high. We arrived in Natcha, and occupied two houses, two single houses.

What we didn't know was that those houses belonged to captains from the Polish army. Yeah, they were two brothers. We occupied the two houses. The captain's families lived in each of the houses, a wife and children. Having them in the houses saved our lives. Nobody came. This was very surprising. Not even the *pastukh*, the shepherd boy, who took away the cattle in the morning, came. So it was understandable that everyone in the neighborhood knew those houses were occupied. But as far as we could see, there was no other movement of people.

We felt very safe in the houses and kept an eye on the families. When one of us was watching, the other two were asleep. We knew we were surrounded by the Polish, but nobody opened fire, nobody came to the house. But you knew they were watching you.

In the evening when we left the houses, we noticed right away that there was a big movement in the bushes. We decided not to go further. We thought we should try to go back. In trying to go back, we passed by a farmhouse and saw from afar that there was a guard in front of the house. We sneaked up and grabbed the guard. We took away his rifle. The guard told us this was the headquarters of the White Polish army. The White Polish were worse to us than the Germans, but we had no dynamite, no ammunition, to blow up the house.

So we just took the guard with us. We wasted a lot of time schlepping him, because he didn't want to go, and he was very slow in walking. We didn't want to kill him. So we had to stay a day at the farmhouse, the headquarters of the White Polish army. He went to sleep in the kitchen by the oven. At the end of the day as we got ready to leave, we saw a farmer running with a pail in his hand. He was screaming something we couldn't hear. Still, we came alert.

Sure enough, there was a truck with German soldiers driving up. We had been watching the main roads, but they came from the back. One of our boys jumped through the window and ran toward the bushes. They killed him because they came from the back.

For me was open only one way, the main road. There was a hill maybe three kilometers long without even one bush. No place to hide. And no strength to run. Up the road I went. They were shooting at me like a target practice.

I can still see the hill, and no place to hide, not even a bush. I still hear the sound of the bullets hitting the ground. Boom, boom, boom. Stlip, stlip, stlip. And thank G-d....

What can I tell you? G-d was watching over me again. Bullets ripped through my coat down by my feet. I had two bullet holes by my sleeve underneath my arm. The soldier's coat had been like brand new, and it was very big. When I finally came back to the base it had six bullet holes through it.

Once, it was in the spring of '44, that we went for food. We went looking for flour, but found only grain. On the way back we stopped by a mill where they made flour from the grain. We left the grain at the mill and said we'll come tomorrow morning to pick up the flour.

Three of us went back to the base with the six wagons and six horses. We unloaded the food: potatoes, cabbage, meat, but we had to bring the wagons back to the farmer. We usually didn't keep the wagons or the horses. We released the horses at the edge of the jungle and the horses made their way back to the farmers. But not this time.

No one was happy to leave the grain and return for flour. This was the only time we have ever left grain, but there was no flour to bring back. The plan was to drive the six horses and wagons across a river, and then go to the mill to pick up the flour. You needed only one horse and wagon to bring the flour back, so we planned to release the other horses. They would go home by themselves and the farmers would pick them up on the road.

We came to the river. There was a valley down the hill, then the river and then another hill to go up the other side of the river. From there, the road to the mill began.

We checked the horses, making sure all the straps were tight before we crossed the river. On the other side there was a little clearing at the bottom of the hill. We checked the horses again, to make sure they were tethered to the wagons, and we went. We were ready to drive the wagons up the hill. The three of us were each driving two wagons tied together. I guided one horse with the wagon, and the next horse and wagon was tied up behind my wagon. Behind me were the other four wagons.

Until you came up the hill, you didn't know what was going on at the top of the hill. I was the scout, the first one to reach the top of the hill. I couldn't believe my own eyes. As far as I could see there were White Polish soldiers each with the eagle, the shiny eagle, the big eagle, on their helmets. Maybe at least one hundred twenty soldiers were lying all around.

They started to fire.

I say to myself, "What are you doing here? Do something!" As I sat on the wagon, I threw my feet over my head and tumbled off the wagon. Before I hit the ground, I saw already my two horses collapsing, falling down, killed. If a fly had been in the air it would have been killed. My feet got tied up in the horses' reins.

I said to myself, "How long are you going to stay here? Untie it, shoot and run!"

So I untangle my feet and pick myself up. I tried to shoot but the first shot doesn't shoot out, so I had to try again. It is a bad bullet. Really, G-d is standing over me. I am standing in the road, opening fire, with shooting all around, and I cannot move. Maybe it is the two dead horses that protect me from the bullets. Then I tell myself, "Run, stupid, run. Don't stay here!"

I get up with my machine gun and spray bullets right and left, and then I start to run. If this had been the Olympics, I would have won a gold medal. I jumped from that place down the hill at the speed of a bullet. But as I was flying in the air, somebody shot off my cap. I was stupid enough to stop and pick it up. My coat had four bullet holes in it, but I came out of it with not even a scratch.

I met one of the other two drivers a few years ago at a Vilna reunion. He came over to me and reminded me of this story. He asked me if I had remembered. I said, "How could I forget it!"

He said, "I was the one lying on the top of the hill shooting at them so you could come back to us."

So we crossed the river on foot, the two other wagon drivers and myself. From that spot I saw, coming from the right side, a big movement, a fast movement. Some White Polish soldiers were running toward us. The closest way to escape would be to the right, but because some soldiers were running there, I led the way to the left. We hurried into the jungle, and eventually came home. We met a group of partisans who had been on the way to the mill, but they heard the shooting and returned to the base. They had already told Fanya, "Your husband is dead. Nobody could survive such gun fire." I rushed to see her, to make sure she knew I was alive.

Near the beginning of June 1944, five of us were called to the shtab, the headquarters. Beside our commander was the most powerful political officer of the Lithuanian Communist Party. We were given orders to take three forty-pound packages of dynamite and, "Not to come back until it is used up!" The order was we shouldn't blow up bridges. "Save the bridges, blow up the trains, but save the bridges."

The front was getting closer. Fewer and fewer trains traveled at night. There were more patrols, more soldiers guarding the railroad tracks.

Our orders were to head west towards Grodno-Warsaw, about one hundred fifty kilometers away. There were many heavily armed German and White Polish soldiers patrolling the train tracks. We had to blow up trains, not tracks, and definitely not bridges. It was difficult to blow up trains in the daylight because you could be seen from a great distance. It took us six days to blow up the first train. Days later we blew up two more.

Finally we could make the long journey back to our base. We walked three hundred kilometers in three nights. We crossed five different rivers, and used ten different guides for short distances to avoid contact with the White Polish army. We arrived home to our base around noontime on the twelfth of June. I took off my boots for the first time in two weeks. In no time my feet got so swollen I could hardly walk.

We received an order that the following day, June 13, we were marching on Vilna. We arrived outside Vilna in the evening and were ordered to rest and sleep, but none of us could. The smell, the stench from the hill near us was unbearable. This was the hill of Ponary.

The fight for Vilna started two days later between the White Polish and the German army. Since it was clear that the Germans were being defeated it was important for Polish pride to have its army take back Polish territory. Every night the commanders listened to the radio. Shablinski told us the news. Abrasha told us also. He listened to both the Russian and the British broadcasts. The opening of the second front, the D-Day invasion, was not known to us until about the twentieth of June.

Finally, finally we had the beginnings of hope.

Chapter 7: Picking Up the Pieces

Vilna was liberated in July of 1944. The Polish army came into the city from the north. We came from the side of Ponary. The smell from the burned bodies, the dead, the killed, it made us all sick. The only thing we wanted was *nekome*, revenge. When we met the Russian army, they needed scouts to bring them across the river and around the city. I was the first one to volunteer. I was one of the scouts who led the Russian army across the small streams and the winding Vileika River into Vilna. I was with the Russian army for four days. The Russians came from the east, but they held back to let the Polish army enter Vilna first. The Russians were happy to let the Polish army fight against the Germans. On July 7th, 1944 the Russians entered Vilna.

When the Russians came into Vilna the Polish soldiers stood there in the streets. Right away the Russians took away all their rifles. A lot of the soldiers were put on big *krushevikes*, trucks, and taken away. Even more Polish soldiers were rounded up on the north side of the Vilia River, loaded into railroad cars and sent to Siberia.

My parents were dead. Fanya's parents were dead. Most of my aunts and uncles and cousins were dead. My parents were killed in Ponary.

When Lolkah and I left the ghetto, Vera's husband had come to lead my father and mother and Yechial to Vera's house, but a Lithuanian police officer saw him talking to my father, so Vera's husband was arrested for talking to a Jew outside the ghetto. Vera's husband was put in prison for thirty days. I saw him after the war so I found out. My family wasn't able to get to Vera's house. My father was taken to a concentration camp, and later to Ponary. My mother went to Ponary.

My mother was in a line. The Germans were separating people; to the right was the labor camp, to the left was death. My mother was walking with Jenke, Lolkah's wife and Jenke's two-year-old daughter Goldie. My mother told Jenke, "Give me your daughter so you will live," and she did. And my mother with Goldie walked to left, and Jenke walked to the right to the labor camp. And Jenke survived the war. I am happy Jenke survived, but it is very hard for me, very hard. I've been to Israel. Yechial has told me about Jenke; that she remarried and has a family, and I am happy for her, but I cannot go see her. There is a jealousy in my heart, that one should live and one should die. It's not right. I am truly happy for her, but it is hard for me.

There were 60,000 Jews from Vilna before the war. Only 800 survived, only 800.

When I first came back to Vilna I was in rough shape. My first job was to be a police officer. I was assigned to guard a bank located next to the offices of the Tzecka Party, the Lithuanian Communist Party. My job was to protect the people coming and going from those offices. After my third day of work I couldn't walk. The doctor put me in the hospital. I was paralyzed on the right foot. I didn't know that I had to report to the police department that I was sick and in the hospital. I didn't do this, so the police had on record that I was a deserter, that I left my post. I couldn't tell the police I was sick because I was already in the hospital. I was there for three days, from the 31st to the 2nd of the next August. But I wasn't issued a food card for the new month because the police thought I was deserter. I escaped from the hospital because they didn't feed me there. I had no card.

I hauled myself home and was so tired, I fell asleep. Now Fanya came from work. She had a job as a secretary in the offices of the Lithuanian Communist Party. "What are you doing here? You're sick. What are you doing here? Go back to the hospital."

I said, "They don't feed me."

"I'll bring you food. You go back to the hospital."

So I walk dragging my right foot from the house back to the hospital. I'm filthy. I haven't showered in a week. In the street I meet a whole group of people. I see one of the commanders from the partisans. This is Yorgis, the Secretary of the Communist Party. Two of his guards stood to block my way. Yorgis is dressed in a black suit. He doesn't even know me. I curse him, "*Yope-twah-yoh-mite*. You son-of-a-bitch. Now when you're dressed like a prince, you don't recognize me? You don't recognize me? I am Grisha Barisovitz. You don't recognize me? You knew me when you were wounded and I schlepped you on my back, when I schlepped you to the wagon!"

One of the two soldiers, a little lieutenant, pulls out a gun. Yorgis doesn't say anything to me, but whispers to the lieutenant. The soldier puts his gun away and they walk on.

Slowly I dragged myself to the hospital because I couldn't straighten up my foot. But two or three hours later, when I came to the hospital I was so tired I fell down and slept. I was hungry, and I was tired. I think I was crying. And that's the way I fell asleep.

But when I woke up, the little lieutenant boy, the bodyguard from Yorgis, was there. "I'm looking for you. This is a present from Ziman."

"Who is Ziman?" I asked.

He said to me, "You don't know Ziman?"

"I never heard of Ziman."

"Do you know the name Yorgis?"

I say, "Yes, Yorgis. I know it."

"It's the same person and he is the secretary of the Tzecka Party."

Just as my name was Hirshka Varshavtchik and I went by the name of Grisha Barisovitz in the jungle, Ziman went by the name of Yorgis. I never knew and I had cursed him, the Secretary of the Tzecka Party, in front of everybody.

The lieutenant brought me this box as big as a dining room table; with food, goods, cigarettes, crackers, bread, and cake. The lieutenant had delivered all the goods in a limousine that was parked outside. Unbelievable. Yorgis called the doctors. The doctors told him what I needed—injections of calcium. They didn't have it in Vilna. Yorgis sent a car to Koenigsberg, which had just been liberated, to get some for me. As soon as they gave me three or four injections, I was like a brand new man.

Another thing Yorgis did was to have an electric generator installed in front of the hospital. This allowed me to have electrical treatments and the x-rays to be done correctly. Whatever I needed he took care of me. And when I came out from the hospital, Yorgis hugged me and kissed me.

Fanya and I had a small apartment. I went to see the old house. All the furniture was there, just the way we left it, that was the way we found it. Nobody lived there. The bakery was just the same way as we left it. Nobody touched it. It wasn't used.

Yechial and I went to Antonovitch. He took all our clothes when we were in the ghetto, and gave not even a needle or thread in return. We went ready to kill him right there. The priest, Ksiadz Jankowski, who helped my family, came to us at Antonovitch's house. Someone had phoned him to tell him we were there. Ksiadz Jankowski told us, "Don't punish him. He was punished. He had two daughters, two beautiful girls who went on a vacation where he had the farmhouse and they both drowned." So he says, "G-d punished him already."

Vera, our housekeeper, still lived in the same apartment with her husband. They went to Yorgis and brought me a document for her husband to state that he helped the partisans. I filled it out because he did help us. He sent us medicine. The document was from the Communist Party.

In October Yorgis called Fanya to his office. Fanya was a telephone operator in the Communist Party's office. Yorgis worked upstairs. He had just gotten off the phone with Fanya's brother, Grisha, who had called from Tula, in Russia. Grisha had seen Fanya's picture in *Krastnoarmeniets*, The Red Army Soldier, a magazine, and he recognized her face. A Russian photographer had taken pictures of the liberation of Vilna. Fanya's picture was taken with Sonya Burstein. Grisha started to holler, "This is my sister, this is my sister!" He got in touch with the C.K. Party, the Central Communist Party in Vilna.

I was working in the Torf Corporation, the Ministry of Mines. From the minister of the Torf, I borrowed his round stamp, and stamped out about 20 blank papers, *camonderofkas*, traveling papers. I wrote out the paper that Fanya was being sent from Vilna to Tula, where her brother was, to bring back a telephone operating system. She would travel from Vilna to Tula. The war was still on in different parts of Europe. To get on a train was just impossible. But two weeks after Yorgis told Fanya about her brother she was on a train headed for Tula. This was in November of 1944.

She baked a honey cake. She held it level in her hands. A general came by and said, "Little girl, where are you going?"

"I'm going to Tula to see my brother," she answered.

"What is in your hand?"

She said, "A honey cake. I baked it for him." He took her onto the train and he gave her a *coopay*, a traveling berth, all for herself, and that's the way she came to Moscow. She took the train from Moscow to Tula. Fanya's brother was the director of a musical school. When she came to her brother in Tula, his students didn't let her in to see him. They said, "Wait. Gregorowitch

Zaharavitch Raichel sleeps until ten o'clock. It is only 9:30, so you have to wait half an hour."

And when Grisha heard it, he laughed, "This is my sister!"

Grisha came to visit us in Vilna. I bought him a tuxedo with a shirt, with shoes. But most important, I went to a Polish family, a gentile house, where we knew his violin was kept in hiding. Before he died, Fanya's father asked this family to hide Grisha's violin and other things. We came with a machine gun to this house. We didn't ask for the clothing, or the linen, or the other things Fanya and Grisha's father had given to the family to hold on to. I had to put the gun against his throat to have him show me where the violin was. Finally the gentile gave it to me. I had to do it, it was Grisha's livelihood.

Fanya and I planned to move to Tula to be with Grisha. Yechial, my younger brother, was part of Abba Kovner's group. He wanted only to settle in Israel. Yechial tried to get to Israel through Rumania. We couldn't get in touch with him.

After my brother left, the Russian authorities wanted to know where he went and why. The Russian political commander, Diddiallise, the same person who arranged Nathan Ring's death, had the police come to my house at 11 o'clock at night to bring me in for questioning. Diddiallise asked me only one question, "Where is your brother?" At the time I didn't know, so I could only tell him that. For three weeks straight, night after night he called me to ask.

I was still working with Torf, the Ministry of Mines. They gave us a brand new truck covered with a special yellow canvas. It was a beauty. The order was, if the truck wasn't being used by the company, and a government worker needed it, I could lend it out. The truck was at my disposal. Because of this order, I gave the truck away every night for people to go pick up supplies; wood, torf bricks, salt from Latukis, the headquarters from grocery supplies; all kinds of supplies, though mostly it was fuel to burn for warmth. Those who borrowed the truck were Jewish workers who worked there in the Latukis. They loaded it up with supplies, and sold it to a pre-arranged buyer. Some drove the truck to Bellarus, just outside Lithuania. The driver came back with two hundred rubles, sometimes three hundred rubles. It was very little pay, but it was extra money.

It happened that one time, the driver of the truck who was not Jewish, but Polish, was registered to leave Vilna on the next evacuation train to Poland. He was going to return to his home. He wanted to make an extra dollar for himself. So he loaded up the truck with the salt, and drove off with the two customers who had paid for it. He drove them out from the warehouse, stopped by the roadside and said, "Look, I have to do something. You stay here, I'll be right back."

He let them off the truck and then drove away. He came to the Holtz market, where he had already another two customers waiting for him, who also had already paid him for the same truckload of salt. He put them on the truck, and he did with them the same thing, the same trick. He said get off, I have to fix something, and again he drove away.

He drove to a friend's house, they had a few drinks together, and he went to look for a new customer. He came back to the same marketplace where he took the second set of customers. He came there, and the prior customers recognized the truck because of the yellow canvas. They started hollering in Polish, *"Ta machina nas obrabowala!"* This truck took away our money!

There were a few policemen at the market. They looked around at what was going on. The customers pointed to the truck driver that robbed them. So the police went after the driver. The driver saw the police and started to drive away. They were on motorcycles and he was with a truck, loaded with three tons of salt. Anyway, he made a sharp turn and hit a lamppost and the truck got stuck.

The driver ran away, but the truck with the salt was left there on the street. The truck was registered to my company. I was the one who signed the papers authorizing the use of the truck. By the time the police officer came to tell me about it, it was about nine o'clock in the evening. I couldn't do anything. I didn't know what to do. So we went to look for Fifke Di Pomele, the former pickpocket who helped smuggle handguns into the ghetto, because he was now a policeman with very good ties to the police captain from this precinct. But Fifke Di Pomele was in Kovna that day and I couldn't reach him.

I didn't want to go to Yorgis. I was ashamed. I didn't want to ask his brother either. Yorgis had two brothers. One was the District Attorney of the Republic of Lithuania, the head attorney. The other brother was the head of the newspaper. I didn't want to go to the district attorney to ask for help. So I said I would hide. I'd see what was going to happen.

The next morning, we were sitting in the house and a lot of friends came in to the house because they found out about the truck. Tefka Szeres, Alka Kremer, and Grishka Gurwicz were among the friends there. They said, "We'll see, we'll wait. We'll see what the police will do."

Sure enough, as we sat there having breakfast, we heard a knock on the door. I wanted to get up and leave the room to go in a different room. Grishka went to the door and opened it up. There was a man in civilian clothes. He asked, *"Vwarning jhareshiv-e-oat?"* The janitor lives here?

"No, he's across the street," Grishka answered and waved to me with the hand like it was nothing. "Somebody is looking for the janitor."

Then the man asked, *"A Varshavtchik shayshivert?"* Does a Varshavtchik live here?

Grishka said, "Yep."

I wanted to jump through the window, but thank G-d I didn't, because I just saw on the ground floor, in front of the doorway, there were two policemen with machine guns. Grishka stepped backwards into the room; his face was as white as paper. So I moved fast. It was a big room, but I rushed to the door. I opened the door all the way and hid behind it to let the civilian in. He stepped inside and I snuck behind his back and closed the door behind him from the outside. I was in the hallway, still not sure what was going on. I stood behind the door and listened.

And there I heard, Fanya say, "Da, da, Yes, I am his wife."

So then I knew the police were after me. I went out to the back door by the kitchen, to the yard, saying to myself, "I'll take a look again."

I walked outside. A little drizzle had begun, and I was wearing only a shirt. I went out from the yard, made a left, and then another left.

I came in front of the house, to the entrance of our building. There I saw the two police with machine guns, standing guard in front of the door. A block, or two blocks away from me, a friend of mine, Motke Shames lived. He had been a partisan. I walked to his house.

Motke Shames said, "You can stay here. We have to go to work, but you stay here."

Motke and his girl friend went to work, and I sat in his house. But I had to send word to my wife to tell her where I was. So I decided I'd go out and take another look to see if they were still watching my house. I walked out and there I saw Motke Shames' father. He was already retired. But he was afraid to stay with me in the house. He didn't want to risk getting in trouble so he waited outside.

"Okay," I said to him. "I'm going away from here. I don't want to put you in to trouble. But just go tell Fanya where I am. Tell her I was with you, and tell her I'm going to try to go to the priest. I'll try to go to the church. And if not, I'll let her know. In the meantime, I'm going to the church."

So he went to Fanya and gave her the message. I walked to the church; I came to the priest, to Ksiadz Jankowski. At times, he was like a father to us. The church was across the street from where we had lived, on Zawalna Street. Now we rented a room on Yagaylonska Street. I made my way to the church and he took me in. He gave me a room with a very soft bed, with a feather pillow, and a down blanket. Everything was starched. He put a pail for going to the bathroom so I didn't have to go out of the room. Later, a nun brought me soup and a loaf of bread.

I hid there for two weeks until the head of Letukis, the headquarters of the groceries, straightened things out. Everything was straightened out with the Jewish workers there—the ones who were selling the salt, loading up the truck with the salt. The headquarters stopped the search warrant for me.

That gave me a chance to get away, to leave Vilna and go to Poland. I don't know how much money the Letukis paid to have the police stop searching for me. The Letukis did this to protect themselves, because if the Russian police caught me I would have to tell from where I got the salt.

The Letukis, the headquarters from grocery supplies, offered me money. I didn't take any money from them. I just wanted to have the papers so Fanya and I could go safely to Poland. They paid for the papers with my name changed, whatever had to be done that I should be able to leave Vilna. And that's what they did. And that's how I became Reischer. We wanted to have Fanya's family name, Raichel, instead of Varshavtchik, but that was the way they made the papers. And that was the last set of papers the man had. Period. The last set. The last paper. He wrote Reischer instead of Raichel. And that's the way I have been going since then.

That was the beginning of November in 1946.

The day before we got on the train to evacuate Vilna to Poland, the priest, Priest Jankowski knocked on the door. He entered and showed us a telegram addressed to him. It said: "Yechial Varshavtchik lives in Italy." Chasia, Yechial's wife, sent the telegram.

We left Vilna in November of 1946. From Vilna we went to Poland. From Poland we walked on foot across to Czechoslovakia. On Christmas Eve we came to Prague. From there we went to Vienna. In Vienna we were going to stay in the Rothchild House, a hotel, but we couldn't because we didn't have proof of marriage. Since we had no papers with us we got married again in Vienna.

We were trying to go to Italy to find Yechial. Everybody was going to Germany, but we had to go to Italy. That's why we had to do so much on foot. Many Jews were returning to Germany to go to refugee camps. There they got clothes, they got room and board, and they got food.

We crossed the *Zebbering*, the Alps, on foot, in the winter, in the snow, on foot. We had to walk, not to the first, but the second railroad station, because the first station had a lot of police there. I don't remember the name of the town, but it felt very good to finally arrive. We were very, very tired. We just lay down at the railroad station on the cement floor and slept.

We arrived in Italy in January of 1947. We took the train to Milan. It was a passenger train. There were many displaced Jews on board, but it was a regular train. We came to Milan and we had an address, Via Unione. We knew we would find help on this street. It was a needle in a haystack, but the policeman saw right away that we were displaced persons. We didn't speak Italian and we had no money. We didn't know anything about what was going on in the world. We talked in gestures and told him, "Via Unione, Via Unione."

He stopped the trolley, told everybody to get out, and then told the trolley driver to drive us to Via Unione, "As close as you can."

Yeah. That was our introduction to Italy. That was beautiful.

At Via Unione the first person we saw was Jashka Kagan. He took us to a rooming house. We lived in the rooming house for months. Korsha Italia Six was the address. It was run by a German woman, Mrs. Hoolrickh. We had to get married again in Milan.

In Italy, I went to work. Starting in February, we worked for the Brichah. The Brichah was a branch from the future Israeli government. There was no Israel yet.

For a long time we hoped to settle in Israel. I wanted very much to be with my brother. At one point it looked as though we could go by ship. We sent all our clothes. Just before we were to leave, the Brichah told me that Fanya would go on the ship LaSpetzia, but they wanted me to stay because they had more work for me to do in Italy. So Fanya stood on the wharf, and she was saying to herself, "What am I doing by myself? You know, where am I going to go? I'm going by myself and I really don't want to do it."

There was a pregnant woman who wanted to get on the ship and there were no more seats, and she wanted to go to her husband who was already in Israel. So Fanya decided to give up her seat to this woman.

I was really mad, but she said she just had a feeling she shouldn't go. It turned out this was the last ship to get through to Palestine before the British sealed the border. Sure enough, when we came home there were the papers from my uncle so we could go to the United States. And again we needed to get married, this time in Rome; so that our exit visas would say we were coming into the United States as a married couple.

Fanya and Hirshka Varshavtchik
This photograph was taken in Italy to be sent to Hirshka's uncle in America.

We arrived in the United States in October, 1948, with a visa. My uncle, already here in America made out an affidavit, an invitation for us. He signed that he was going to support us for the next five years. We came to port in Brooklyn where he met us. We stayed with him for one week then moved into our own apartment.

To think that we survived. To think of all those who did not. Never in my wildest dreams did I think we would survive. I would never have thought it possible.

Epilogue

I am very close to my father. My father has allowed me into his inner circle of friends, a circle of his fellow survivors. Often when I've been thinking of him, he calls. And when the telephone rings, I usually know before answering, he will be on the other end of the line.

During Rosh Hashanah, my grandparents came. In spirit they came. On the first day of the Hebrew New Year 5766, (October 4, 2005) at Kehillat Lev Shalem, The Woodstock Jewish Congregation, my grandparents, all four of them, had come. My grandparents who had been killed at Ponary, for whom I light the memorial Yortzeit candles each Yom Kippur, had come. With near to one thousand people singing, chanting prayers, silently introspecting, my grandparents had come, and I broke down in tears. With my wife holding my hand, while my children watched, wanting to console me, yet unable to do so, I wept, sobbing uncontrollably. For a long time I cried. In a semi-circle my grandparents stood before me, looking down on me. Silently, my grandparents admonished me. And I understood. The writing of this book was taking too long.

Soundlessly I told them that it was painful to look back. Imagine, I told *them* it was difficult. They knew I had avoided my father's story for months on end. They knew I preferred the safety of writing fantasy tales where I could keep my favorite characters from harm. They understood, but still, I needed to finish this work.

I told them, "I will." And I cried with an aching heart, a tightness in my chest as if my ribs would break.

I watched as my father told his story, recording his words on tape, to be transcribed later. He was calm, his eyes were clear. With the telling, he left me and traveled between worlds, between then and now. He spoke for minutes at a time, telling a particular story.

After the telling, he returned to the present, to me. We laughed at times. And at times we almost cried. I asked questions to spur on memory, to fill in details. Only once did my father pause, and then steer clear of the question. Only when I asked him to speak of his parents, and Ponary. He couldn't speak. He closed his eyes and looked away.

I wished I hadn't asked.

Listening to his story I didn't notice the verb tenses. It was only in the second reading of the transcript that I realized my father would inevitably switch from past to present tense. I wondered at this and even edited many of the verbs. At least I did so initially. Many more of those present tense verbs have been edited by the publisher's proof reader to make for an easier read. But know, as the memory became more intense, my father moved from past to present tense as he spoke.

To commemorate *"Kristalnacht"*, The Night of Broken Glass, the beginnings of Nazi violence on November 9, 1938, we went as a family to our synagogue in Woodstock. The author of *Forging Freedom*, Talbot Hudson, came with the book's hero Jaap Penrat, to speak of the Holocaust. In words and pictures, Jaap's courageous deeds are conveyed by Talbot Hudson. Jaap Penrat smuggled out over four hundred Jews from France. After Talbot Hudson's talk, Jaap Penrat spoke, still with a heavy European accent. He looked at the audience with clear, still eyes. At times though, his gaze was distant as he spoke. Whenever Jaap came to an intense part of his story he switched verb tenses, just like my father, from past to present. I was taken aback. I wondered if this was a European mannerism in the telling of a story.

After his talk I walked up to Jaap Penrat. I waited as he answered the children's questions. He paused for a drink of water. Finally, I asked, "Do you see these memories often? I noticed that you spoke in the present tense."

His eyes opened wide and he stared at me, measuring me. "I see them every day, and it is horrible!"

I shook his hand and thanked him for coming. I thanked him for his deeds during the war as well. I felt so inadequate. How could I thank him enough?

Jaap Penrat answered the question I couldn't bear to ask my father. Like Jaap, when my father looks back, he relives his memories so vividly, his broken world of Vilna becomes the present for him.

As a child growing up, I didn't have enough time with my father. He worked long and hard. He drove a taxicab twelve hours a day, six days a week. He opened a series of small businesses in which he worked seventy to eighty hours a week. As a grocery store owner, he left home at four in the morning and returned at six o'clock in the evening, only to eat dinner and go to bed.

My father worked hard for many reasons, many of them good. He helped raise a family, sent his three sons to college, and even bought an automobile for each son. He gave to us whatever he could afford. His children and wife always came first. My father never wanted or needed anything for himself. Never. Finding him a gift has always been an almost impossible task.

However, I know he also worked to avoid the past. If he could put his whole attention on work, and exhaust himself with twelve hour work days into a deep, deep sleep, allowing his body to recuperate for the next day's effort, there would be little time for idle thoughts, for remembrances of life before America.

And last of all, my father worked out of desperation. He had survived. One of his brothers had not. His mother had not. His father had not. Most of his aunts and uncles had not. His wife's parents had not. His world had been shattered. He even had to change his identity. Learning eight languages was not enough. He still needed to learn English once he finally stepped onto American soil.

My father had survived.

Part of the reason he works so hard, even now, even though he is retired, is because he wishes he could have saved his own parents, his brother, his aunts and uncles, his wife's parents, his cousins, his friends, his neighbors…and he feels the weight of not having been able to.

Though he tried, my father could not have saved everyone. The very fabric of his life was torn asunder. He was overwhelmed, but he managed, somehow, to survive. He has gathered what pieces of life he could find. Bit by bit, he has done what he could to repair the rent, to heal the wounds, and to weave a new life.

And because we've talked, my father and I, because he has let me into the forbidden realms of his heartbreak, I've come to know a part of the pain he sees every day, he feels every day.

My wish for my father, my prayer for my father, is that he come to accept the limitations of what he could do, of what could be accomplished in that hell through which he survived, and that he come to a deep and abiding peace with himself. *"Ken yehi ratzon."* May it be the desire of the Holy One.

www.ingramcontent.com/pod-product-compliance
Lightning Source LLC
Chambersburg PA
CBHW030524100426

42813CB00001B/143